The Trial of the Catonsville Nine

THE TRIAL
of the Catonsville Nine

by Daniel Berrigan

FORDHAM UNIVERSITY PRESS
New York
2004

Library of Congress Cataloging-in-Publication Data
is available from the Library of Congress

Printed in the United States of America
08 07   5 4 3

Fordham University Press edition, 2004
First published by Beacon Press, 1970

Grateful acknowledgment is made to Atheneum Publishers
for permission to quote from *The Investigation* by Peter Weiss,
copyright © 1966 by Jon Swan and Ulu Grosbard,
copyright © 1965 by Suhrkamp Verlag (Frankfurt am Main);
and to Grove Press, Inc., for permission to quote from
Selected Poems of Pablo Neruda edited and translated
by Ben Belitt, copyright © 1961 by Grove Press, Inc.

Photographs of David Darst, Thomas and Marjorie Melville, Mary Moylan, George Mische, and John Hogan courtesy of Bob Fitch; photograph of Thomas Lewis courtesy of Phillip Marcus; photograph of Daniel Berrigan courtesy of Jack Eisenberg; photograph of Philip Berrigan courtesy of Ted Polumbaum (Life Magazine, © Time Inc.).

CONTENTS

"I Had No Right"
Lyrics by Dar Williams

God of the poor man this is how the day began
Eight codefendants, I, Daniel Berrigan
Oh and only a layman's batch of napalm
We pulled the draft files out
We burned them in the parking lot
Better the files than the bodies of children

I had no right but for the love of you
I had no right but for the love of you

Many roads lead here, walked with the suffering
Tom in Guatemala, Phillip in New Orleans
Oh it's a long road from law of justice
I went to Vietnam, I went for peace
They dropped their bombs
Right where my government knew I would be

I had no right but for the love of you
I had no right but for the love of you

And all my country saw
Were priests who broke the law

First it was question, then it was a mission
How to be American, how to be Christian
Oh if their law is their cross and the cross is burning

The love of you
The love of you

God the just I'll never win a peace prize
Falling like Jesus
Now let the jury rise
Oh it's all of us versus all that paper
They took the only way they know who is on trial today
Deliver us unto each other, I pray

I had no right but for the love of you
And every trial I stood, I stood for you

Eyes on the trial
8 a.m. arrival
Hands on the Bible

PREFACE TO THE FORDHAM
UNIVERSITY PRESS EDITION

I sat in the Hungarian Coffee Shop across from St. John the Divine in New York City waiting for Dar Williams to walk through the door. She said to look for light-brown, shoulder-length hair and someone who was short. I described myself as tall with light hair, but that fit half the women here. It didn't matter, I knew her when I saw her, from some unconscious memory of a photograph no doubt. I asked her to meet me because I wanted to know how she came to write "I Had No Right," the song on the *Green World* album (and the epigraph for this book) about Daniel Berrigan and the Catonsville Nine. I had worked out that Dar must have been two years old when nine Catholic activists walked into the draft board office in Catonsville, took the files outside, and burned them with what Dar calls "only a layman's batch of napalm." After talking to Dar for a little while, the answer to my question was obvious. She spoke easily about having to heal the earth, about making the world a better place. These ideas rolled off her tongue with a familiarity that made it obvious they were things she thought about every day. The Catonsville Nine wanted peace. They wanted to stop the bloodshed in Vietnam, and they were willing to put their freedom at stake to do it. They wanted to change the world. So does Dar.

Tracking the footprints left by *The Trial of the Catonsville Nine* on its journey through our culture in the last 35 years has been an encounter with artists, poets, academics, filmmakers, performers, and activists, both Catholic and secular, and many others who have found inspiration, hope, and outrage in its words. Daniel Berrigan, poet, teacher, and Jesuit priest, chose to write a play. He gives voice to each person on trial for this action, and they are powerful, truthful voices that continue to speak through his prose. They inspired Dar, a young singer/songwriter over thirty years later, to write, "Tom in Guatemala, Philip in New Orleans / It's a long road from law to justice." Like Dar, many have been willing to travel that road with them. They offer inspiration and hope to people who meet them for the first time, either in these pages, on stage, in performances, or in the film and documentary the play also inspired.

For Dar, writing and performing her song has led to a wealth of experiences and stories from people, her fans, or someone they knew whose life was touched by the story of *Catonsville* and the pull of nine people who demonstrated their extraordinary commitment to peace. One of Dar's fans wrote her a letter explaining how introducing "I Had No Right" to a friend evoked a story, a connection, and a history that tied her to the Berrigans. In a tale of six degrees of separation, she writes that her friend was so inspired by the song "that she dug up some old photographs of an evening back in 1968 shortly after Dan was released from jail (for the first time!)." A local community group in Syracuse was producing the play. "It was very late at night, and Dan walked through the door . . . you can imagine the looks on their faces!" As I read the letter, I marvel at the careful script of the longhand written on lined yellow paper. The letter is undated, but it was delivered backstage at a Town Hall performance in New York City in June 2003, along with three photos. The old black-and-white pictures show a just-released Father Berrigan sitting on an elevated wooden floor, cross-legged, surrounded by the actors, some on the floor in front of him, some sitting behind in the rows of old theater seating. They look tired and cold. They all wear coats. All listen intently.

Daniel has visited many acting groups doing the play over the years, but there were many times he could not get to performances. In 1975, he was invited to attend a production of the play in Japan. But he had to abandon his plans to go to Tokyo after the Japanese government turned down his request for a visa. In May of that year, Dan received a call from a cast

Daniel Berrigan makes a surprise visit to the cast at the Salt City Playhouse in Syracuse, New York, 1968. Photo by Merton Gordon, delivered to Dar Williams by Kate Newburger at Town Hall, June 2003.

of performers in Galway, Ireland. Knowing it was his birthday, they wanted to wish him a good one. The strong desire to reach out speaks to the way the play creates community, especially for the actors who assume the roles that give public witness to the harm done by their government's policies.

Gordon Davidson was the first to direct *The Trial of the Catonsville Nine* when it opened at the Mark Tapper Forum in Los Angeles. The play won an Obie and led to the off-Broadway production in New York City. *Catonsville* caught the attention of Hollywood legend Gregory Peck, who turned it into a movie. The Pecks invited Father Berrigan to attend the film's showing at Cannes, and since he was no longer behind bars at the time, he accepted. Like the play, the movie still finds an audience so many years later. A 2002 review of

the film appeared on Amazon.com, noting the "powerful performances" in a film that lacked the contemporary production
values of a commercial blockbuster.

Thirty years after the event, film of the Catonsville action
was pulled out of a TV cameraman's basement. For fear of the
FBI, this visual record had been locked away and never shown
until filmmaker Lynne Sachs featured the black-and-white
images of the draft files burning in her 45-minute film, *Investigation of a Flame* (2001, First Run/Icarus Films). The experimental documentary was listed as "One of the ten best films
released in 2002," by Phillip Lopate in *Film Comment*. The
way *Flame* is described reveals how prescient the Catonsville
action remains in a country still defining itself by war and
death. "With Daniel and Philip Berrigan leading the way, this
powerful, imaginative statement of protest reveals the neces-
sity to reflect actively on our government's wartime forays into
the lives and politics of other nations." The remaining members of the Catonsville Nine, interviewed for *Investigation of a
Flame*, continue to draw viewers by the power of their convictions. Jessica Winter, of *The Village Voice*, described them as
"humble architects of this purposeful yet scathingly meta-
phoric act of civil disobedience." *Investigation of a Flame* aired
a number of times throughout the month of September 2003
on the Sundance Channel, and it continues to appear there
occasionally.

The play sustains each new generation. It speaks to young
people open to the possibilities of changing the world, able to
sustain a vision of peace, and willing to travel the road that
leads to that new place. When the students at Fordham University performed the play in the spring of 2003, they had only
two weeks to rehearse; a President's Day snowstorm delayed
some cast members from returning to campus. But by opening
night, they knew their lines. Kristen, the student who played
Marjorie Melville, told me how assuming Melville's character
seemed natural. Kristen had seen *Investigation of a Flame*
when it was shown at the Museum of Modern Art in New York
City two years earlier. "Her words expressed so well how I
actually felt," said Kristen. Melville had previously inspired
Kristen when she was asked how it felt to be a woman partici-

pating in the Catonsville action. Kristen describes the woman she would later play, saying, "I loved her reaction. She said she was part of a community. It's not a male/female thing. It's a group of concerned Christians doing what they think is right." These voices challenge so many boundaries, both cultural and legal, ones carefully constructed by a nation seeking to protect its own interests. As the students performed a play whose sentiments they felt mirrored their own in the present, Father Berrigan attended the last performance. There he finally met the mother of one student who had invited him to her college over thirty years ago when she was an undergraduate. He never made that speaking engagement because he was still imprisoned.

As the play is passed from one generation to the next, it is the threat of a good example that makes these nine people so powerful, and the powerful so nervous. Their refusal to acquiesce to a militarized society kept both Dan and Phil Berrigan behind bars for long stretches. The first time Philip Berrigan was able to see *The Trial of the Catonsville Nine*, it was performed in German. For years, frequent jail terms had prevented him from attending the performances, and when he finally managed to be in the audience, he was surrounded by West Berliners. It had become the official play of the German Green Party and was produced in venues throughout the country in the 1980s. Neither Philip nor Daniel could attend the New York off-Broadway performances; they were both in jail at the time. Filmmaker Lynne Sachs interviewed Philip Berrigan for her documentary between Philip's many prison stays. Patrick, the Fordham student who played Thomas Melville, was jailed after his own act of civil disobedience at a protest in front of the School of the Americas, the same place that trained those responsible for killing six Jesuit priests in El Salvador in 1989.

The play has been out of print for years, yet the requests to reproduce it come with a constant regularity. *The Trial of the Catonsville Nine* continues to be used as a course text, and it is performed frequently around the country. One request from the Lutheran School of Theology in Chicago dated August 2003 reads, "I would like to produce a staged reading sometime this year. It is a stirring call to Christians to act on their beliefs and is particularly meaningful in the current climate of war, hate, and fear."

This new edition by Fordham University Press has been changed only slightly. Father Berrigan rewrote various passages to make the language more inclusive, more accurately reflecting the diversity among those who have long resisted war-making.

The Trial of the Catonsville Nine is part of a culture of resistance and wisdom, though rarely openly celebrated. As Dar Williams recounts her experiences performing the song, she has come to understand that the Berrigans and the spirit of the Catonsville Nine are always with us. They are part of the foundations of this culture, "You realize that people know them, and to mention them brings that to the surface. They are always there, part of a shared culture." Their spirit of hope and resistance is a living collective memory, one that challenges and threatens the makers of war and its weapons. It is time to bring that unconscious memory back into the open and celebrate the power of these words.

—Robin Andersen

INTRODUCTION

The trial was finished, the judge's gavel had pounded us into true shape, and the thing was done, lost, given over, run like veins aground; in the shape of the body, in the shape of man.

The facts of the case are perhaps known by now. "An F.B.I. agent estimated that at least 600 individual draft files were in the two huge wire baskets carried by nine defendants from local board number 33 in Catonsville, Maryland, on May 17, 1968, and set afire in a parking lot" (A.P. Wire). The trial evidence brought forward a more modest figure of ruin: some 378 files. In any case, the damage was something more than symbolic, as the judge insisted several times. The damage exceeded $100, and the prosecution proved it to the hilt. So our crime stood under a Federal statute.

The trial of the "Catonsville Nine" was held in a Baltimore Federal court, October 5–9, 1968. A verdict of guilty was returned against each defendant on each of three counts: destruction of U.S. property, destruction of Selective Service records, and interference with the Selective Service Act of 1967.

In composing this book, I have worked directly with the data of the trial record, somewhat in the manner of the new "factual theater." As I understand it, that form requires essential adherence to the letter of a text (in this case, some twelve hundred pages, supplied to us by the court stenographer). I have been as faithful as possible to the original words, spoken in the heat or long haul of the trial, making only those minute changes required for clarity or good sense.

In condensing such a mass of material, it was predictable

that a qualitative change would occur, almost by the law of nature, as the form emerged. And this of course was my hope: to induce out of the density of matter an art form worthy of the passionate acts and words of the Nine, acts and words which were the substance of the court record.

It was not however a matter merely of a record. It was a matter for us of life and death. For each of us, the spring had wound tight in the weeks of discernment and scrutiny and long, patient sharing which preceded Catonsville. There was a danger that intensity and passion would be dissipated in the routine of the trial itself, in the obeisance paid to legal niceties and court routine, in the wrangling and paper shuffling which threatened to obscure the firmness and clarity of the original deed.

This work had but one purpose therefore: to wind the spring tighter.

I have reduced all the principals of the trial, with the exception of the defendants, to anonymity. The defense counsel, who are our friends, will not be chagrined by this treatment. The judge and prosecutors have their own kind of fame, elsewhere. It is extremely dubious that I could do anything to add to it. Where evidence overlapped due to common experience (Philip Berrigan, Tom Lewis), or where special circumstances intervened (Marjorie and Tom Melville, the only married couple in the group), I have altered the text in accord with what I understood to be dramatic exigency.

The tone of that exigency is of course more easily sensed than described. How to convey the tenderness of Marjorie Melville, the gentle simplicity of John Hogan, the anguish of Tom Lewis, brought into court from jail each day, remanded to jail at the end of each exhausting session? The air of the court was charged with grandeur, with damnation, with bathos. Spite, blindness, danger, gentleness, the interplay of wit and dim wit, an overriding sense that here, in one place, almost against our will, by choices that bore us headlong, the tragic ingredients of the war were being pressed into a single concentrate. Was it named hemlock?

It was my impossible, almost despairing, task to attempt to evoke something of all this.

Six months before the short journey to Catonsville, I had gone half way around the world to Hanoi, on a mission to repatriate three American prisoners of war. I had cause to remember, after our crime, the virtue commended to us by our hosts in North Vietnam. It was strangely enough that of patience. "A revolutionary virtue," they called it—those men who of all men of our century should by rights know. And I have questioned myself in the year since our trial; is it possible, having endured a Federal trial and, six months later, a state trial (held in despite of double jeopardy), enduring a limbo of travel restriction and limitation of speech —is it possible that in being more patient than the warmakers, we might become peacemakers? We could only try. We could be patient with the judge, with the prosecution, with the Federal marshals, with one another (we would learn the cost of that); patient also with the students who marched for us, who went home from our trial fervent and turned around; and then promptly forgot or repudiated us within a few months.

Cornell, where I had been teaching and counseling for two years, came quickly to its own torment, after sharing to some degree in mine. The students who traveled to Baltimore by the hundreds in October put us down sharply a few months later: our style, our nonviolence, our religion. The spring of 1969 brought the hour of decision closer to home; the atmosphere was hottening up, a torrid zone. The war that had no end, the police repression, the immobile, marmoreal establishments (those Maginot Line Eminences!). And then the response: seizure of a building, hit and run, anger, inner division, threat of sabotage. The *Cornell Sun* (no tongue of revolution it!) saluted my *hutzpah* a few days before the trial. But by June, I was old hat.

My brother Philip said, when we talked of these things: "There is no one way, there are as many ways as there are men or communities. It is up to us to pursue our way as best we know how, and to respect theirs."

His remark had a Buddhist flavor. About methods in such times as these, no one knew. We improvised our lives as we went along. To be sure, we had certain insights, having to do with community and nonviolence. We had come upon them in the course of a long loneliness, a long exposure, a long defeat, as conditions worsened around us, and the light sank lower.

But we could be reasonably sure of one thing, in the midst of great and general perplexity. That is to say, we had not sleepwalked toward Catonsville, nor toward the trials that followed. We went into court as we had gone into the draft center—wide awake, neither insane nor amnesiac.

And that might be something, that might offer something. We had had no part in social madness. We knew (how simple and crucial a thing) our own names, where we came from, why we were on trial, the direction we had chosen to follow. We knew who our brothers were, and what our duty was to them; all the truths denied to American consciousness, by wars running hot and cold, and by peace, another word for war. We knew who we were; we could at least claim that. We had not dismembered our brothers on a universal autopsy slab. And having no part in that murderous operation, perhaps we could re-member man, perhaps we could surgically and lovingly put him together —according to the image of God, according to. the law of life, by which the healer is healed in the very act of his art.

Yet an ominous sense of the future weighs upon me, as these words go to press. The war continues, inexorably. Will this record, the first of its kind to be published since the war began, also be the last? It well may be. The time of taking risks and submitting before the judicial system is drawing to a close. The war machine, which has come to include the court process that serves it, is proving self-destructive. The courts, like the President (two, three Presidents), like the Congress, are turning to stone. The "separation of powers" is proving a fiction; ball and joint, the functions of power are fusing, like the bones of an aged body.

Indeed it cannot be thought that men and women like

ourselves will continue, as though we were automated he-
roes, to rush for redress from the King of the Blind. The
King will have to listen to other voices, over which neither
he nor we will indefinitely have control: voices of public
violence and chaos. For you cannot set up a court in the
Kingdom of the Blind, to condemn those who see; a court
presided over by those who would pluck out the eyes of men
and call it rehabilitation.

Summer 1969

The Trial of the Catonsville Nine

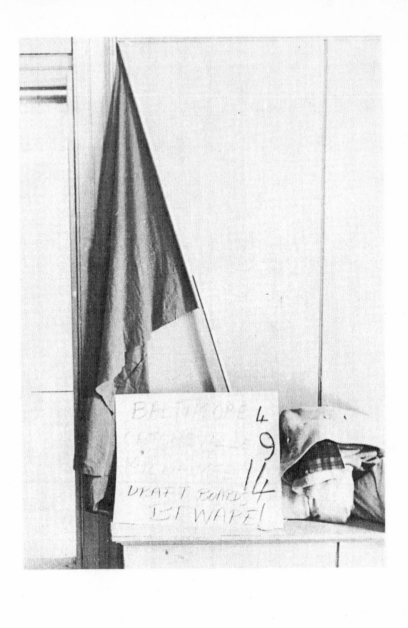

Brother David Darst
In Memory
(1942–1969)
Because the work
was finished
in that flare.

Toward the end of our second session in Moscow,
the Russians produced a cable.
Zhukov read: The Baltimore Federal Court has
just sentenced members of the Catonsville Nine
to as much as three years in prison.
Zhukov: These nine are courageous champions of
peace, working in difficult conditions. Our
conditions here are quite different. We are free
to engage in our work.
Fay Knopp: I am very appreciative of the cable
you read us. Many of these people are our dear
friends. You must also have heard of the Mil-
waukee Fourteen. Also in our society, we refer
to the Moscow Five. We are proud of these people
in both our countries, who go to jail for justice
and principle. I should not like to forget the
Moscow Five, and the others in this country who
are punished for speaking out. They are martyrs
also and we honor them in our society.
Kharkhardin: The Moscow Five I regard as a
group of idlers and parasites who got away with
less than they deserve.
Meacham: I do not believe they are idlers or
parasites. I believe they are men and women who
are providing your children and mine with
strength and freedom that one day will find its
fulfillment.

NEW YORK TIMES MAGAZINE; MARCH 9, 1969

1

The Day of a Jury of Peers

DEFENSE

With regard to jury selection, we wish to make one brief statement, your honor. The defendants will not participate in any way in the selection of the jury. That will be a matter between the court and the U.S. attorney.

JUDGE

You do not wish to have the benefit of striking out names you object to?

DEFENSE

We do not wish any strikes whatever. We are abstaining completely from the jury selection.

JUDGE

Very well. All I am going to do is to be sure I get the names. I am now going to do a little housekeeping. Bring in the prospective jurors. Swear them in.

(The prospective jurors are brought in.)

Members of this panel, in this case the United States government, by indictment, has commenced a prosecution against nine defendants. The indictment charges in three counts the following offenses:

That the defendants did willfully injure and commit depradation against property of the United States; did willfully and unlawfully obliterate records of the Selective Service System, Local Board No. 33 located in Catonsville, Maryland; and did willfully and knowingly interfere with the administration of the Military Selective Service Act of 1967, by removing and burning the records of Local Board No. 33 located in Catonsville, Maryland, and by disrupting the official activities at the location of the Local Board No. 33.

The indictment further charges that the defendants aided and abetted one another in committing these alleged offenses.

Each of the defendants has pleaded innocent to these charges. Accordingly, the burden of proof is upon the government to prove the guilt of any of the defendants beyond a reasonable doubt. Now I want to ask each of the prospective jurors some questions.

Mr. Starlings, what is your position?

JUROR

I work for the National Security Agency.

JUDGE

Do you feel that your position in the government would make it difficult or impossible for you to do equal justice between the government and the defendants in this case?

JUROR

No, sir.

JUDGE

You may step down.

Mr. Jones. You served in World War I?

JUROR

Yes, sir. I was in the Army, American Expeditionary Force, World War I.

JUDGE

Have you been active in the American Legion or other activities since? Have you taken any position with respect to protests against the Vietnam war? Have you taken any public position on that war?

JUROR

No, sir.

JUDGE

You may step down. . . .

Mrs. Kilmurray, you say that at one time you worked for the Department of Defense?

JUROR

That is right. I was the Chief of Position Classification at the U.S. Army at Edgewood Arsenal.

JUDGE

Do you feel that your experience in that job would make it impossible, or would make it difficult, for you to do equal justice between the government and the defendants in this case?

JUROR

No, I do not. . . .

JUDGE

You may step down.

Mr. Seidel. I believe that you answered "yes" to the question that you had served in the Armed Forces.

JUROR

Yes, sir. It was in the Second World War.

JUDGE

Have you taken any position, any public position, with respect to the war in Vietnam?

JUROR

No, sir.

JUDGE

You may step down. . . .

Mrs. Smith, you answered, I believe, that you are now working for the Federal government?

JUROR

Yes, as a management analyst with the Army.

JUDGE

Is there anything about your job, or anything about your experience, or any other reason at all, which you feel would make it difficult for you to do impartial justice between the government on the one side, and the defendants on the other?

JUROR

No, sir. . . .

JUDGE

You may step down.

Mr. Buchanan, you were, I believe you said, in the military service at some time?

JUROR

Yes, sir.

JUDGE

During what conflict was that?

JUROR

The Korean War and the Cuban crisis.

JUDGE

Do you feel that your experience in the service would make it difficult for you to do equal justice?

JUROR

No, sir.

JUDGE

You may step down.

State your name, sir.

JUROR

My name is Eric Smith, Jr.

JUDGE

Mr. Smith, you say that you are the branch chief of the Department of Defense at Fort Meade?

JUROR

Yes, sir.

JUDGE

Are your duties classified, or can you tell me what the branch chief does, what you do?

JUROR

I am an industrial engineer in charge of construction and space allocation for the National Security Agency and the Department of Defense.

JUDGE

And you served in the Armed Forces heretofore in one of the conflicts?

JUROR

I have served in the Armed Forces, yes, sir, during Korea.

JUDGE

Would your experience as a former Military Policeman make it difficult for you to decide this case fairly?

JUROR

No, sir, I don't think it would influence or bias my opinion. . . .

JUDGE

You may step down.

Mr. Austin, you have served in the military?

JUROR

World War II for three years, 1942 to 1945, in the U.S. Navy.

JUDGE

Do you know of any reason why you would not be able to decide the case solely on the evidence?

JUROR

No, sir. I am a very conscientious person.

JUDGE

I hope all the jurors will be. You may step down. . . .

Mr. Raymond Steer. You have served, I believe, in the Armed Forces?

JUROR

I started with the 29th Division here at Fort Meade, and I switched to the Air Force.

JUDGE

Does anything in your experience make it difficult for you to do justice in this case?

JUROR

No.

JUDGE

You may step down.

Mr. Johnston, have you served in the military service?

JUROR

I was in the Army, yes, sir.

JUDGE

What branch?

JUROR

Well, I was on active duty in the Army, then I was in

the Army Reserves, and I was at the rank of Sergeant E–5 when I got out.

JUDGE

You may step down.

Mr. Bergman, you have a contract with the government, is that right?

JUROR

Yes, sir. With NASA.

JUDGE

And you also were in the Armed Forces?

JUROR

Yes, sir.

JUDGE

Is there anything about your experience in the Army which would make it difficult for you to do justice between the government on the one side, and these defendants on the other?

JUROR

I do not believe so.

JUDGE

Are you prejudiced in any way, for or against the defendants, and the position they have taken?

JUROR

Well, I believe I have already formed an opinion, sir.

JUDGE

I think we have run into difficulties here. You may be excused. . . .

Mr. Fanzone, you have been in the Armed Forces?

JUROR

I served three years in the U.S. Army, from 1961 to 1964.

JUDGE

Would anything make it difficult for you to do equal justice here?

JUROR

No, your honor. . . .

JUDGE

Mr. Davis, you have served in the Armed Forces?

JUROR

Yes. I was in the U.S. Navy in World War II, between 1943 and 1946.

JUDGE

Would anything in your experience in the Navy, or since, make it difficult for you to do equal justice between the government on the one hand, and these defendants on the other?

JUROR

No, sir. . . .

JUDGE

You may step down.

Are the government and the defense ready to have the jury sworn?

PROSECUTION

The government is ready.

DEFENSE

We are ready.

JUDGE

Swear the jury.

(*Whereupon the jury was sworn and seated.*)

2

The Day of the Facts of the Case

WITNESS

We had just come back from lunch. A gentleman came up the steps. I looked at him, and I said: "Could I help you, sir?"

Before I could say anything else, all of these people came in.

I asked them not to come in. I begged them not to come in the office, but they did.

I was so confused and upset at that point. They utterly terrified us. We were just terrified.

Of course, they immediately went to the files. I noticed one gentleman was carrying a trash burner.

I begged them not to take the files. I begged them. One of them went right over to the files, and I could see him read the label on the 1–A Qualified drawer.

He just emptied all those sheets right into the trash burner.

I begged them and pleaded with them, but it was to no avail, and I might say that I have never been treated with such bad manners in my whole life, and with such disrespect or uncharity.

JUDGE

Strike it out. The defendants are not being tried for their manners.

PROSECUTION

What happened after they emptied the drawers?

WITNESS

I took hold of the trash burner, and I tried to pull it

away, but I could not get it away from them, naturally. And in the scuffle I cut my leg and my hand.

Then they ran down the stairs. I followed to the edge of the building and saw the fire, and I came running back up, and I said to the girls: "My God, they are burning our records."

PROSECUTION

And the 378 files taken would include all information necessary to draft young men?

WITNESS

That is right, everything that concerns a man.

PROSECUTION

What effect on the functioning of Local Board 33 has the incident of May 17 had?

WITNESS

It has given us a tremendous amount of work, and it certainly has inconvenienced our boys.

PROSECUTION

Have you yourself done any work in restoring those files?

WITNESS

I would estimate that in the general reconstruction, getting the papers from the Armed Forces, making lists, reconstructing the cover sheets, writing them all up again —all of this—I would estimate that, myself, alone, I have spent at least eighty hours. The other clerks spent about forty hours working with me. We also had three supervisors from State Headquarters working for three weeks.

PROSECUTION

Have you finished reconstructing these 378 files, as of today?

WITNESS

No, sir.

DEFENSE

Mrs. Murphy, at the time of the action about which you testified, what did the several people who came into the office say to you?

WITNESS

There was a lot of conversation: "We don't want to hurt you. We have no intention of hurting you." Some of it was about the war in Vietnam; that this is not a good war, and that we shouldn't be there. One of them said: "You send boys away to be killed." Father Philip Berrigan told me he didn't want to hurt me, and I am sure he meant it.

DEFENSE

Can you remember this having been said: "Don't fight." "We don't mean you any bodily harm." "You are helping in the deaths of American boys."

WITNESS

That is right. Yes, I remember that, sir.

DEFENSE

When you speak of an injury you received, would that be an injury for which you treated yourself with a Band-Aid?

WITNESS

Well, I went to the doctor, really, because it was—I suppose it was maybe, superficial. But I was very, very, very, very much upset. Mental anguish, I had.

DEFENSE

Would you conceive that the prime purpose of the files, and the work you do, is to serve the government?

WITNESS

Yes, sir, the Army of Defense. I am part of the Army of Defense.

DEFENSE

Mrs. Murphy, did not some of the defendants while in jail send you flowers and candy?

PROSECUTION

Objection, your honor.

JUDGE

We are not trying the manners of the defendants, neither their good manners nor their bad manners. We are trying a specific charge.

DEFENSE

No more questions.

3

The Day of the Nine Defendants

THE TRIAL

Supersonic time
that noses the ether
like a hell hound
on mercy and bombing missions
bore me here
dropped me like a dud

I sit in the town stocks
for ten thousand years
a judge's or butcher's scrawl
GUILTY around my neck.

On a park bench in Japan
a man's shadow sits
after the bomb's wink
ten thousand years

until God wink again
like a lucky fisherman
and the man's mouth snap
shut on the hook they say
God says stands for hope

The man screams or yawns
unheard from as a fish
or a man at rope's end
by Goya or Daumier

DANIEL BERRIGAN

PHILIP BERRIGAN
I am a member of a family including six boys
All of us were born in Minnesota
My father was railroading out there
and he married my mother   who was a German immi-
                                        grant
I think perhaps some influence on my life
came from these days
Minnesota was pioneer country
We lived on the Iron Range
Most of the people were Scandinavians   Finlanders
Swedes and Norwegians
I remember my older brothers telling at great length
of the struggles they had
to survive in the bitter winters
We were poor
I remember the depression years very well
I think those years had some bearing
on the inclination my life was to take
I think this is true of my brother Dan as well
and other members of our family
We lived with people
and accepted them as they were
During the depression years I remember my mother
welcoming people from the road
There were many men in those days traveling the roads
impoverished and desperate
Even though we did not have too much to eat

she never refused them
This made an early and deep impression upon us
DEFENSE
Will you indicate what your early education was?
PHILIP BERRIGAN
I come from a devout Catholic family
our early years were more or less stereotyped
All six boys went to parochial school
about two miles away
We had to walk both ways and pack our lunches
We were educated by nuns
in a rather harsh and authoritarian environment
We graduated from a Catholic high school
I went to work and tried
to save a little money to go to college
I was inducted into military service
after one semester of college
I underwent training in the Deep South
first in Georgia and later in Florida
and North Carolina
I was perceptive in a dim sort of way
noticing the conditions of Black people
in the rural areas where we trained
I noticed
and remembered
the dire poverty we encountered
One time when we were out on maneuvers
we happened to be trying out the rations
that would be fed us overseas
The climate was very humid and oppressive
and we were famished
at the end of the day
We came upon some Black people
who were selling whole chickens for $1 apiece
We had some money along
Five or six of us
bought chickens and ravenously ate them
Then a white boy came along

grinned at us   Said we had been eating
not chicken   but buzzard

DEFENSE

Did you experience any of the war in Europe?

PHILIP BERRIGAN

I spent about a month
in the British Isles
I saw the devastation of cities
a result of the great German air raids
Bristol   Coventry   Sheffield   London
I think I should add
in all candor
I was an enthusiastic participant in World War II—
in contrast   of course to my present attitude
which arose because of the influence of people
who have surrounded me

DEFENSE

What happened after your discharge from military service?

PHILIP BERRIGAN

I entered the Society of Saint Joseph
for training
toward the priesthood
I lived with Black seminarians
I learned from them
in a graphic way
what it means to be Black
in this country

DEFENSE

Where did you go after ordination?

PHILIP BERRIGAN

To New Orleans to teach
in a Black high school

DEFENSE

Did you participate in the social struggles then going on
in the South?

PROSECUTION

Your honor, how long are we going to go on?

' ' ' ' ' ' ' ' '

*God forbid we should be twenty years without a rebellion.
What country can preserve its liberties if the rulers are not
warned from time to time that their people preserve the
spirit of resistance?*

THOMAS JEFFERSON
"LETTER TO GENERAL WILLIAM S. SMITH
NOVEMBER 13, 1787"

, , , , , , , , ,

PHILIP BERRIGAN
    Very early   in New Orleans
    I became deeply involved
    in the civil rights' struggle
    We did voter registration work
    We worked with the poor
    in the slums of New Orleans
    We tried to provide
    some sort of bridge
    between the Black and White communities
    We tried to attack racism at its roots
    We tried to open minds a bit
JUDGE
    We are not trying the racial situation in the United
    States, nor are we trying the high moral character of this
    witness.
PHILIP BERRIGAN
    At any rate
    I began to investigate
    what was called the Cold War
    I began to study
    how nuclear weapons were engineered
    and gotten ready for "duty"
    on both sides

‘ ‘ ‘ ‘ ‘ ‘ ‘ ‘

FRANZ

*The century might have been a good one, if man had not
been watched from time immemorial by the cruel enemy
who had sworn to destroy him; that hairless, evil, flesh-eating
beast—man himself.*

*Perhaps there will be no more centuries after ours. Per-
haps a bomb will blow out all the lights. Everything will be
dead—eyes, judges, time. Night. O tribunal of the night, I
have taken the century upon my shoulders and have said: I
will answer for it. This day and forever.*

SARTRE: THE CONDEMNED OF ALTONA

, , , , , , , ,

There was a loosely formed group
of peace people
operating on the campuses
I did some work with them
after President Kennedy's assassination
When the bombing of North Vietnam started
we began a peace organization
We were doing very unsophisticated
and unthreatening things
in those days
We were trying to get a forum on the war
trying to get people to listen
But I remember the fierce opposition
even to this
Anyone who spoke out against Vietnam
was apt to lose his coattails
I lost mine
I was transferred to Baltimore
by my superiors
because of my peace activity
The Catholic community in Newburgh
where I had been teaching
was distraught by what we were doing

I was ordered by my superior to keep silent
But then Pope Paul
spoke at the United Nations
I considered this a mandate
to open my mouth again

DEFENSE

What was the nature of your peace activity in Baltimore?

PHILIP BERRIGAN

We always tried
to gauge our activity
in terms of the reality of the war
We started with prayer vigils
with meals of reconciliation
with a few tentative marches
in downtown Baltimore
We began to demonstrate   at military bases
We went to Fort Myers   Virginia
(Fort Myers is the home
of the Joint Chiefs of Staff)
We tried to contact men
like General Wheeler
and General Johnson
former Chiefs of Staff of the Army
to tell them of our concerns
to sit down with them
citizen to leader
The military were immune
from any citizen influence
They were a law unto themselves
General Wheeler ignored our letters
So we went to his home
and demonstrated outside
We were forced to leave
We came back in a month's time
and were forced out again
The third time   we were forcibly ejected
Apart from these attempts
I also tried continually

to keep in touch with the Congress
I made a proposal to Senator Fulbright
suggesting it might be a good thing
to investigate the war
in light of the moral opinion of the nation
We planned to bring a team
of theologians   to testify
before the Foreign Relations Committee
Fulbright was partial to the idea
but he never had political leverage
particularly from the churches
so of course our idea died aborning.
At Christmas of 1967
I also spent two hours
with Secretary Rusk   I went to his office
with another clergyman
We discussed all aspects of the war
He was very gracious
but he did not tell us anything
he had not said before
and that was not enough for us

DEFENSE

Are there any books that influenced your thinking on the
war in Vietnam?

PHILIP BERRIGAN

I was influenced by my reading
on both sides of the question
I have read all the authors
on the Vietnam war
including those who wrote
in support of the war

DEFENSE

I would like to have this book, *In the Name of America*,
marked for identification. Father Berrigan, I show you
Defendant's Exhibit No. 5. And I ask if you have read
this book?

PHILIP BERRIGAN

Yes I have

DEFENSE
> Did this book influence your thinking as to the legal aspects of the war in Vietnam?

PHILIP BERRIGAN
> Yes it did

DEFENSE
> I want to make a formal proffer. The book *In the Name of America* has to do with the reasonableness of the defendant's view.

JUDGE
> The government has agreed on the sincerity of his views.

DEFENSE
> The government did not agree as to the reasonableness of his views.

JUDGE
> In that case, I must question the prosecution. Does the government contend that the reasonableness or unreasonableness of the defendant's view has any bearing on the issue of intent? You had better think that over carefully. . . .

(The prosecuting attorneys consult.)

PROSECUTION
> Your honor, we say that a reasonable man could have the defendant's views. . . .

DEFENSE
> Your honor, the defense has scored a capital point. This is the first time in a trial of this nature that such an admission has been made by the government. But we shall return to this matter later. . . .
>
> Father Berrigan, I ask you: did there come a time, then, when you began seriously to consider civil disobedience?

PHILIP BERRIGAN
> Yes   I came
> to the conclusion
> that I was in direct line

with American democratic tradition
in choosing civil disobedience
in a serious fashion
There have been times in our history
when in order to get redress
in order to get a voice   vox populi
arising from the roots
people have so acted
From the Boston Tea Party
through the abolitionist and anarchist movements
through World War I   and World War II
and right on
through the civil rights movement
we have a rich tradition
of civil disobedience

DEFENSE

Now, the action for which you are being tried here was
not the first such action you were involved in. To state it
briefly: seven months earlier, in October 1967, you along
with the defendant Thomas Lewis and two others not
present poured blood over Selective Service records in the
Baltimore Customs House.

PHILIP BERRIGAN

We were prepared
for the blood pouring
because we had practiced civil disobedience
in Virginia
In fact my brother and myself
had practiced civil disobedience for years
by signing complicity statements
in support of draft resisters
So four of us took our own blood
and when the equipment for drawing our blood
broke down   we added animal blood
We attempted to anoint these files
with the Christian symbol of life and purification
which is blood

DEFENSE
Will you explain why, with a jail sentence staring you in
the face, you felt impelled to act again at Catonsville?
PHILIP BERRIGAN
Neither at the Customs House   nor at Catonsville
do I wish my actions reduced
to a question   of acquittal or conviction
Rather I   and all of us
desire to communicate
with the bench   with the prosecution
with our country
We have already made it clear   our dissent runs counter
to more than the war   which is but one instance
of American power in the world
Latin America is another instance   So is the Near East
This trial is yet another
From those in power we have met
little understanding   much silence
much scorn and punishment
We have been accused of arrogance
But what of the fantastic arrogance   of our leaders
What of their crimes against the people   the poor and
                                          powerless
Still no court will try them   no jail will receive them
They live in righteousness   They will die in honor
For them we have one message   for those
in whose manicured hands   the power of the land lies
We say to them
Lead us   Lead us in justice
and there will be no need to break the law
Let the President do   what his predecessors failed to do
Let him obey the rich less   and the people more
Let him think less of the privileged
and more of the poor
Less of America and more of the world
Let lawmakers   judges   and lawyers
think less of the law   more of justice
less of legal ritual   more of human rights

To our bishops and superiors we say
Learn something about the gospel
and something about illegitimate power
When you do   you will liquidate your investments
take a house in the slums   or even
join us in jail
To lawyers we say
Defend draft resisters   ask no fees
insist on justice   risk contempt of court
go to jail with your clients
To the prosecution we say
Refuse to indict
opponents of the war
prefer to resign   practice in private
To Federal judges we say
Give anti-war people   suspended sentences
to work for justice and peace
or resign your posts
You men of power   I also have a dream
Federal Judges   District Attorneys   Marshals
Against the War in Vietnam
You men of power   you have told us
that your system is reformable
Reform it then
and we will help
with all our conviction and energy
in jail or out

David Darst (center) with arm around friend

DAVID DARST
　　I was not in the room
　　when the files were taken
　　Perhaps I could be called
　　the lookout man
　　If anyone came to stop us
　　I was to hurry in
　　and let the others know
　　One might have called it
　　a Bonnie and Clyde act
　　on behalf of God and ourselves
DEFENSE
　　Do you recall the substance with which the records were
　　burned?
DAVID DARST
　　They were burned
　　with a kind of crude napalm
　　We made it from a formula
　　in the Special Forces Handbook
　　published by the School for Special Warfare
　　at Fort Bragg

‘ ‘ ‘ ‘ ‘ ‘ ‘ ‘

The recruit is led through candles to the image of a saint.
His blood is drawn and sprinkled on the effigy. He then
takes an oath and is required to carry out a murder.

MAFIA HANDBOOK

In emergencies, napalm is made in the following manner.

GREEN BERET HANDBOOK

, , , , , , , , ,

We did not use all the ingredients called for
We made a very crude form of napalm
consisting of two parts gasoline
one part soap flakes
Nor did we cook our mix into a jelly
We left it in liquid form
so we could pour it on the files
We felt it was fitting that this agent
which had burned human flesh
in the war in Vietnam   and in many other places
should now be poured on the records
which gave war and violence
their cruel legitimacy

DEFENSE
Would you explain your intent in acting at Catonsville,
other than destroying the files?

DAVID DARST
First of all to raise a cry
an outcry   at what was clearly a crime
an unnecessary suffering
a clear and wanton slaughter
Perhaps this is similar to the case
of a man in his home who sees a crime
someone is being attacked outside
His impulse   I think   his
basic human impulse
is to cry out   to call for help

‘ ‘ ‘ ‘ ‘ ‘ ‘ ‘

*Dear people of Camardo, I appeal to you for understanding
and forgiveness.*

*I tried to save what could be saved. It was not possible for
me totally to prevent the terrible deaths.*

*I do not want to defend myself. I can only abandon my-
self to God's judgment.*

*I resisted the orders without success. Could I not then
have refused to carry out the order with my last breath, without heed to the most extreme personal consequences?*

BISHOP DEFREGGER OF MUNICH
ON HIS WARTIME ROLE IN EXECUTION
OF ITALIAN VILLAGERS

’ ’ ’ ’ ’ ’ ’ ’ ’

That was one intention
an outcry that   hopefully
would stop the crime
I saw being perpetrated
Another intention was
to halt the machine of death
which I saw moving   and killing
In the same way perhaps
a person in Czechoslovakia
when tanks invade his country
throws bricks into the wheels
of the tanks
and sometimes a puny effort
stops a tank
This was my hope
to hinder this war
in a literal way
an actual physical way

DEFENSE

Do you have any other basis for the intent you have described?

DAVID DARST
> An outcry against the fact
> that our country can spend
> eighty billions a year
> chasing imaginary enemies
> all around the world
> I was living last year
> in a poor ghetto district
> I saw many little children
> who did not have enough to eat
> This is an astonishing thing
> that our country
> cannot command the energy
> to give bread and milk
> to children
> Yet it can rain   fire and death
> on people   ten thousand miles away
> for reasons that are unclear
> to the thoughtful

DEFENSE
> Did your religious belief have any influence on your
> decision?

DAVID DARST
> Well I suppose my thinking
> is part of an ethic
> found in the New Testament
> You could say
> Jesus too was guilty
> of assault and battery
> when he cast the money changers
> out of the temple
> and wasted their property and wealth
> He was saying
> It is wrong to do what you are doing
> And this was our point
> We came to realize
> draft files are death's own cry
> We have not been able

to let sacred life
and total death
live together quietly within us
We have cried out on behalf of life
The government has chosen
to see our cry
as anarchy and arrogance
Perhaps real anarchy lies
in the acts of those
who loose this plague of war
upon a proud people
in face of a great and burning doubt
This doubt cries to heaven
Our cry too goes out
in the name of life
Men around the world hear   and take heart
We are one with them   We believe that today
we are at a joyful beginning   We are together
and we are not afraid

PROSECUTION
You have said elsewhere that draft files have no right to
exist. Do you believe that slum properties have no right
to exist?
DAVID DARST
Slum properties I would say
have no right to exist
PROSECUTION
Would you symbolically burn down slum properties?
DAVID DARST
How could I
symbolically burn down slum properties?

(*Commotion in court. Laughter from the audience.*)

JUDGE (*Gavel. Anger.*)
If we have any more demonstrations, we are going to
clear the courtroom.

THOMAS LEWIS
    Let me speak of an experience
that has bearing on why I am here
As you recall   some years ago
there were civil rights demonstrations
at Gwyn Oak Park   here in Baltimore
The issue was the right of the Black man
to use the park
I went there   to do some sketches
of the demonstrations
When I arrived
they had just arrested some clergymen
You know I had a feeling
that I should be where they were
I was slowly drawn into things
I picketed for awhile
But I was in no position psychologically
to consider civil disobedience
Later I became active
in the Catholic Interracial Council
and in CORE
I was slowly being educated
in the realities around me
My schooling went forward
with my experience
In a sense   I could have been called
a very conservative person
coming out of high school

going into art studies
It is a shocking thing
walking a picket line
for the first time
sensing the hostility of the people   the White people
particularly when we went to suburbia
to demonstrate for open occupancy

DEFENSE

What first motivated you to become interested in the issue of Vietnam?

THOMAS LEWIS

Well there were many factors
It is unfortunate
reflecting on it now
In Christianity   we are taught
that all men are a human family
Yet I was not profoundly moved
about Vietnam
until my younger brother was there
an immediate relative
Of course
in a Christian sense
one's family is much more broad
than the immediate family
The war helped educate me
I began to read and go to lectures
about the war
Of course   on an artist
the visual impact of the war
is immediate

DEFENSE

What opinion did you come to, with respect to the war in Vietnam?

THOMAS LEWIS

I came to the conclusion
that the war
is totally outrageous
from the Christian point of view

But it is not enough   to say this
You know   those terms
have become almost meaningless
The war is outrageous   unChristian
and it is a great deal more than this
DEFENSE
On the strength of these beliefs, did you then engage in
peace activity?
THOMAS LEWIS
Yes   after the speech
of Pope Paul at the U.N.
a group of us
began what we called
the Interfaith Peace Mission of Baltimore
We were a group of concerned people
attempting to express to others
what we felt about the war
We began with a peace vigil
at one of the churches here
We prayed for peace
in response to the invitation
of religious leaders throughout the world
We followed this with a walk
demonstrating visually
our hope for peace
Things progressed   We had visits
with Maryland congressmen and senators
We wrote letters to them   and delivered them
personally   in Washington
We met with silence
from all of them
We met
with hostility and apathy
One of the vigils in Washington
was at the home of McNamara
another was at the home of Rusk
Particularly Rusk indicated
his lack of concern

He said it was not his job
to deal with moral matters
He said
to the clergymen in the group
that it was their responsibility
to deal with the morality of the war
We did not need his homilies
We had been doing that for years
So we turned toward the military
We engaged in conversations
with the military hierarchy
They accepted no responsibility
for the direction of the war
The responsibility was not theirs
They were just taking orders

JUDGE

You said "no response." You mean they did not do what
you asked them to do, is that it?

THOMAS LEWIS

No response your honor
We were standing there   We were speaking
on behalf of the suffering
We were speaking as Americans
We were proud to be Americans
Yet we have representatives in Vietnam
who do terrible things in our name
We were saying to the military
This is wrong   This is immoral   This is illegal
And their response to this was
they were only obeying orders

JUDGE

But they did respond to you, did they not?

THOMAS LEWIS

It was an atrocious response

DEFENSE

You are an artist, are you not?

THOMAS LEWIS

Yes sir

JUDGE
> We are not trying his ability as an artist.

DEFENSE
> Would you indicate, Mr. Lewis, where your work has
> been exhibited? And what prizes you have won?

JUDGE
> This has nothing to do with the issue. We are not trying
> his ability as an artist.

THOMAS LEWIS
> So be it
> I then moved into civil disobedience
> This is a legitimate form
> of social protest   It is well documented
> in Christianity
> Civil disobedience was practiced
> by the early Christians
> The spirit of the New Testament deals
> with responses to one another
> and with a law that overrides
> all laws   The one law
> is the primary law of love and justice
> toward others
> As a Christian
> I am obligated
> to the primary law of brotherhood
> We have responsibilities not only
> to our immediate family
> but to the world

JUDGE
> Yes, you have said that.

THOMAS LEWIS
> So I made a decision to protest
> This protest involved
> the pouring of blood
> a strong indictment of those records
> Blood   in biblical terms
> and in contemporary terms
> is a symbol of reconciliation

related to the blood
that is being wasted in Vietnam
not only American blood
but the blood of the Vietnamese
We acted   Father Phil Berrigan   Dave Eberhart
Reverend Mengel and myself
in Baltimore in October of 1967
For that I received a prison sentence
of six years in a Federal penitentiary

DEFENSE

After the conviction, and while you were awaiting sentence, you also engaged in the Catonsville action, did you not?

THOMAS LEWIS

Yes
It was the response of a man
a man standing for humanity   a man
a Christian   a human being
seeing what was happening   not only
in Vietnam but beyond Vietnam
There was a difference   in my mind   between
the two protests
The draft records
on which we poured blood
were records of the inner city
the ghetto areas
Part   of the protest
was to dramatize that the war
is taking more cannon fodder   from the poor areas
than from the more affluent areas
The symbolism was perhaps clearer
in the second case
We used a contemporary symbol   napalm
to destroy records
which are potential death certificates
They stand for the death of those they represent
who are put in the situation
where they have to kill

But beyond this
napalm manufactured in the United States
is part of our foreign aid
We supply weaponry
to more than 80 countries   We have troops
in more than 40 countries   These troops
are backed up with our weaponry
So I was speaking not only of Vietnam
I was speaking of other parts of the world
The fact is
the American system can flourish
only if we expand our economy
in these other countries
The fact is
we produce more goods than we are capable
of consuming   We must have new markets
We must bring our industries   our way of life
into Vietnam and Latin America
We must protect our interests there
But we asked at Catonsville
Whose interests are these?
Who represents the interests of Latin America?
Who represents the interests of Vietnam?
I was well aware
that in civil disobedience
you take an action
you stand   you are arrested
you attempt to express your views
you are prepared
to take the consequences
The consequence to me
was a six-year sentence
for pouring blood

‹ ‹ ‹ ‹ ‹ ‹ ‹ ‹

GALILEO

If only I had resisted, if only the natural scientists had been able to evolve something like the Hippocratic Oath of doctors, the vow to devote their knowledge wholly to the benefit of mankind! As things now stand, the best one can hope for is a race of inventive dwarfs who can be hired for anything. . . . I surrendered my knowledge to those in power, to use, or not to use, or to misuse, just as suited their purposes.

BRECHT: GALILEO

› › › › › › › › ›

I was aware too that
if I became involved in Catonsville
I would be summoned once more
for trial   This is the trial
and a greater sentence may follow
I was fully aware of this at the time
It was a very thoughtful time
In a sense   it was a choice
between life and death
It was a choice between
saving one's soul and losing it
I was saving my soul

‹ ‹ ‹ ‹ ‹ ‹ ‹ ‹

OPPENHEIMER

We have spent years of our lives in developing ever sweeter means of destruction; we have been doing the work of the military, and I feel it in my very bones that this was wrong. . . .

I will never work on war projects again. We have been doing the work of the devil, and now we must return to our

*real tasks. . . . We cannot do better than keep the world
open in the few places which can still be kept open.*

KIPPHARDT: IN THE MATTER OF J. ROBERT OPPENHEIMER

, , , , , , , , ,

PROSECUTION
Did you consider that others like you might hold a view
about Vietnam that was contrary to yours?
THOMAS LEWIS
Well that has happened
as we all know   I don't see
any of these people in jail
I don't see any of these people suffering
as we are suffering
PROSECUTION
That was not my question. That was not my question.
THOMAS LEWIS
I don't see any of these people
in prison
What do these people represent?
such people
are defending their economic interest
They are defending
their personal interests
They are gaining because of the war
The whole weaponry industry is enormous
because of the war
The Sentinel Missile System
would not be possible if it were not for this war
Who are gaining from the war?
They are an elite minority
who are very wealthy
But what is happening to the poor
in this country?
I am not trying to
belabor the point

PROSECUTION

I think the question could be answered yes or no, could
it not? Yes or no, were you aware that it was against the
law to take records from the Selective Service, and burn
them?

THOMAS LEWIS

I wasn't concerned with the law
I wasn't even thinking about the law
I was thinking of what those records meant
I wasn't concerned with the law
I was concerned with the lives
of innocent people
I went in there with the intent   of stopping
what the files justify
The young men
whose files we destroyed
have not yet been drafted   may not be drafted
may not be sent to Vietnam for cannon fodder
My intent in going there
was to save lives   A person
may break the law to save lives

JUDGE

If these men were not sent, other people would have
been sent, who would not otherwise have been sent,
would they not?

THOMAS LEWIS

But why your honor
Why this?
Why does it have to be like this
You are accepting the fact
that if these men are not sent
other men will be sent
You are not even asking
what can be done
to stop this insane killing
what can be done
to stop the genocide
what can be done

to stop the conditions in Latin America
You are not dealing
with these things
You are accepting this
as in Nazi Germany
people accepted the massacre
of other people
This is insane
I protest this

PROSECUTION

Your honor, I move that all of this be stricken. I don't
know how long he is going to continue.

THOMAS LEWIS

How long?
I have six years Mr. Prosecutor
I have lots of time

‘ ‘ ‘ ‘ ‘ ‘ ‘ ‘

BECKET

*It is not for me to win you round. I have only to say no to
you.*

KING

But you must be logical, Becket!

BECKET

*No. That isn't necessary, my liege. We must only do—ab-
surdly—what we have been given to do—fight to the end.*

JEAN ANOUILH: BECKET

THOMAS MELVILLE

I am Thomas Melville   priest
In August of 1957
I went to Guatemala
My work there was the work
of any Christian minister
trying to teach the people
the truths of the Christian faith
I was not there very long
when I felt I was getting
a little ahead of myself
The material circumstances of the people—
I hesitate to use the word "poverty"
they were living
in utter misery
So I thought   perhaps instead of talking
about the life to come
and justice beyond
perhaps I could do a little
to ameliorate their conditions
on this earth
and at the same time
could give a demonstration
of what Christianity is all about
So we decided we would join
the revolutionary movement
knowing that perhaps
some of us would be killed

Myself   Marjorie my wife
who was a nun at the time
John Hogan   and five others
joined in this agreement
We were all finally expelled
by the American Ambassador
who was recently assassinated
I know you are bored by this

JUDGE

Nobody is bored by this, it is an extremely interesting
story. But we cannot try the last ten years in Guatemala.

MARJORIE MELVILLE

I am Marjorie Melville
wife of Thomas Melville
We first met in Guatemala
We were trying to find out
our role as Christians
Was it to see people's needs
and get involved
or were we to say
Well   this is too difficult
It is too hard to know what to do
Do we stand back
or do we go in
on the side of the people   and say
What can I do to help?
We were in anguish
trying to figure out what to do
with people who needed our help

THOMAS MELVILLE

I put up the title of the church property
so we could get a loan
(without the permission of the Bishops)
I got into trouble for it   I signed the loan myself
There was simply
no organization in the country
that would help the people

JUDGE
    We are not trying the state of Guatemala. We are not
trying the Church in Guatemala.

MARJORIE MELVILLE
    I had been living
    a very sheltered life
    in Guatemala City
    I never went out
    I dealt only with the parents of school children
    Then I took a course
    in Christian social doctrine
    I went into the slum areas
    I began to understand   and to show the students
    what life in Guatemala City was about
    Through working with the students
    I began to realize
    my country's involvement in Guatemala
    Every time we asked for help
    for very simple projects
    like putting water in a village
    or setting up a cooperative
    we found that funds were not available
    Money was always available
    but only in areas
    where the peasants
    were in active despair   Money was available
    so they would stay quiet

THOMAS MELVILLE
    Under one government
    land that belonged to the United Fruit Company
    was distributed to peasants
    But a later President   Castillo Armas
    took the land from the peasants
    and gave it back
    to the United Fruit Company
    There were about 3000 people who did not want to move
    off the land

They were killed or moved forcibly
off the land
JUDGE
We are not trying the United Fruit Company.

‹ ‹ ‹ ‹ ‹ ‹ ‹ ‹

THE UNITED FRUIT COMPANY

*When the trumpets had sounded and all
was in readiness on the face of the earth,
Jehovah divided his universe;
Anaconda, Ford Motor,
Coca-Cola, Inc., and similar entities;*

*the most succulent item of all,
The United Fruit Company Incorporated
reserved for itself: the heartland
and coasts of my country. . . .*

*Then in the bloody domain of the flies
The United Fruit Company Incorporated
unloaded, a booty of coffee and fruits
brimming its cargo boats, gliding
like trays with the spoils
of our drowning dominions.*

PABLO NERUDA

, , , , , , , , ,

THOMAS MELVILLE
I went to the President
Ygidores Fuentes
to ask for land for the people
He had 80 national plantations

He was giving them to his political cronies
He was very courteous
but he said there was
no land for these peasants
They did not have capital
They did not have know-how to work the land

JUDGE

We are not trying the government of Guatemala, nor
the Catholic church in Guatemala.

MARJORIE MELVILLE

The group of students I was working with
chose a name
which in English means "Crater"
because they felt that our spirit
should be like a volcano
which erupts forth love for men

‹ ‹ ‹ ‹ ‹ ‹ ‹ ‹

*The United States should not worry about communists in
Latin America. The communists are no longer revolution-
aries. But the Americans should worry about the Catholics,
who are.*

FIDEL

› › › › › › › › ›

Our superiors
got a little nervous
about our desire   to work with the peasants
and they thought it would be better
if we left the country
before the thing got too big

‘ ‘ ‘ ‘ ‘ ‘ ‘ ‘

The world expects that Christians will speak out loud and clear, so that never a doubt, never the slightest doubt, could arise in the heart of the simplest man.

The world expects that Christians will get away from abstractions and confront the blood stained face which history has taken on today.

The grouping we need is a grouping of men resolved to speak out clearly and to pay up personally.

CAMUS: THE UNBELIEVER AND THE CHRISTIAN

, , , , , , , , ,

We were asked to leave Guatemala
in December of 1967
We went to Mexico
trying to help the peasants
and student leaders
who also had been expelled
Their lives were in danger
Being associated with us put them in danger
In fact I found out
that their names
were on the Secret Police lists
and they would have been murdered
as 4000 people had been murdered
in the last 2 years
It is impossible to describe that

JUDGE
Well, we are listening.

THOMAS MELVILLE
Eighty-five percent of the people of Guatemala
live in misery
You don't live in misery
perhaps that is why
you don't worry about it

They live in misery
because two percent of the population
are determined
to keep them that way
These two percent
are aligned with business interests
in Guatemala
especially with the United Fruit Company
The United States government
identifies its interests
in Guatemala
with the interests of American big business
and with the Guatemalan two percent
who control the country
So if any peasant movement
does not conduct itself
according to their wishes   that is to say
if such a movement
is not completely ineffective
they start screaming
"They are communists!"
and begin executing these people

JUDGE

You mean to say that the United States government is
executing Guatemalans?

THOMAS MELVILLE

Yes   your honor

JUDGE

Has the United States government sent troops into Guatemala?

THOMAS MELVILLE

Yes   your honor

JUDGE

When?

THOMAS MELVILLE

At the end of 1966
and in January of 1967

JUDGE
> And you say that the United States executed people
> there?

THOMAS MELVILLE
> Yes   It was reported
> even in *Time* magazine

JUDGE
> Well, we are not trying the series of Guatemalan revolu-
> tions.

THOMAS MELVILLE
> No   the court
> is quite busy   trying us
> We wanted to participate
> in the revolutionary movement
> We knew it would not look good
> if an American priest or nun
> were killed in Guatemala
> by American Green Berets
> We wanted to complicate things
> for the United States in Guatemala
> because we did not want to see a slaughter
> there   like the one in Vietnam
> There are all kinds of communists
> in Guatemala   beyond doubt
> I was accused of being a communist
> Good people who want a piece of land
> are accused of being communists
> Thousands of them have been killed
> in the last few years
> and I wanted to stop that

MARJORIE MELVILLE
> I did not want to bring
> hurt upon myself
> but there comes a moment
> when you decide
> that some things should not be
> Then you have to act
> to try to stop those things

On my return
I was very happy when I found
other people in this country
concerned as I was
I know that burning draft files
is not an effective way
to stop a war   but
who has found a way
of stopping this war
I have racked my brain
I have talked to all kinds of people
What can you do
They say yes   yes
but there is no answer
no stopping it
the horror continues

THOMAS MELVILLE
We wish to say lastly
why we went to Catonsville
Americans know
that their nation was born in blood
we have expanded our frontiers
and pacified the Indians
in blood

MARJORIE MELVILLE
The creature of our history
is our fatherland today
The history we create today
will form the minds and hearts
of our children tomorrow

THOMAS MELVILLE
I hear our President   confuse greatness with strength
riches with goodness   fear with respect
hopelessness and passivity with peace
The clichés of our leaders
pay tribute to property   and indifference to suffering
We long for a hand of friendship and succor
and that hand

clenches into a fist
I wonder how long we can endure

MARJORIE MELVILLE
We wash our hands in the dirt of others
pointing to the invasions or atrocities of others
certain that our own invasions and atrocities
are more excusable   because more subtle
though indeed far more devastating

THOMAS MELVILLE
We ask this court and this nation today
Will you acknowledge our right
to work for change?

MARJORIE MELVILLE
We do not ask for mercy   we do not ask that history
judge us right   That is a consolation
for more visionary souls than ours

THOMAS MELVILLE
We ask only that Americans
consider seriously   the points
we have tried to raise

MARJORIE MELVILLE
If they do this   we have been successful
our act has been worth the expense   the suffering

MARY MOYLAN

I went to Uganda in 1959
I worked as a nurse-midwife
I also went on safaris
I trained students in nursing
I taught English to secondary school girls
While I was in Africa
I took courses
in African history and anthropology
I was working at Fort Portal
up near the Mountains of the Moon
In the summer of 1965
American planes   piloted by Cubans
bombed Uganda
supposedly by accident
This made me very interested
in our foreign policy
and exactly what was going on
Finally
a serious conflict developed
between myself
and the Administrator of Hospitals
I said that I loved Fort Portal very much
but there were several things I must object to
I felt that the Africans
should have more responsibility
Much of our role   seemed to be
to provide a white face in a black community

I also felt that the students
should have broader training than they were getting
There was a large government hospital
right down the road
It could use our help
The administrator broke my contract
and asked me to leave
I stayed in Uganda for two months
so that I could tell the people
why I was leaving
When I returned home
I became director of the Women Volunteers Association
in Washington D.C.
Through my involvement in Washington
it became obvious to me
that we had no right to speak
to foreign countries about their policies
when things at home were in very sad shape
I was aware of
the militant Black community in Washington
It became obvious that "law and order" is a farcical term
In instances which I know of
the law was broken by the government
In fact justice for a Black person
is just about impossible
It became obvious to me
that our politicians are right
Our foreign policy is indeed
a reflection of our domestic policy
In Washington a Black youth
was shot by a white policeman
A verdict of justifiable homicide
was handed down
I remember too
a protest staged by a young leader
who had a juvenile record
A southern congressman then read
into the *Congressional Record*

this man's juvenile record
This is absolutely forbidden   by law
It was pointed out to the congressman
that his procedure
was illegal   His answer was
I did it once and I will do it again
I think when you see
the imperatives placed on you
by such events at home
by the lives
lost in Vietnam
lost in Latin America and in Africa
then it is time to stand up
This is what it means to be a Christian
that you act on what you say you believe
This is what
Christ meant when He lived
We have not only to talk
but if we see something wrong
we have to be willing
to do something about it
This is my belief
As a nurse
my profession is
to preserve life
to prevent disease
To a nurse
the effect of napalm on human beings
is apparent
I think of children and women
bombed by napalm
burned alive by a substance
which does not roll off
It is a jelly
It adheres
It continues burning
This is inhuman   absolutely
To pour napalm

on pieces of paper
is certainly preferable
to using napalm on human beings
By pouring napalm on draft files
I wish to celebrate life
not to engage in a dance of death

            ‘ ‘ ‘ ‘ ‘ ‘ ‘ ‘ ‘

In dark corners I have heard them say
how the whole town is grieving for this girl
unjustly dealt, if ever woman was
for glorious action done.

ANTIGONE: SOPHOCLES
, , , , , , , , , ,

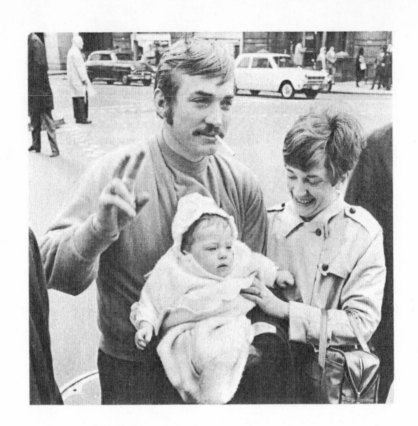

DEFENSE
Mr. Mische, you worked in Latin America for four years?
GEORGE MISCHE
Yes   I worked in Central America
and in the Caribbean
I organized labor groups
housing programs   land programs
We would work up   through the grass roots
I would submit our proposals
to Washington for approval
I went to Latin America
with the idea
that the Latins would be there
waiting at the boat to greet me
because I was an American
That is the naïveté we have   I guess
until we arrive overseas
Then I realized
how wrong I was
We were not only not welcome
now and then we had bricks
thrown at us
This confused me   but
after I became involved
at a higher level
I started to understand
why bricks were thrown at us
I was working in two countries

where revolutions had taken place
I should not say "revolution"
I should say "coup d'état"
military overthrow of governments
Two democratically elected governments
were overthrown by the military
with Pentagon support
At that point   I felt I could not
in conscience go on with this work
because John Kennedy had said
we would not deal
with military dictatorships
At the overthrow of democracy
we would stop all military support
and all economic support
We would withdraw our people
to force the leaders
to return to democracy
Well   when I saw the opposite occur
I resigned   This reversal of things
had most impact on me
in the Dominican Republic
That was such a tragedy
as to be unbelievable
A man like Trujillo
ran that country   for 32 years
When someone dared talk
about social change   or social reform
they would go into his house
take the head of the family   out of the house
cut off his penis
put it in his mouth
cut off his arms and legs
drop them in the doorway

PROSECUTION
I have to object. I am trying to be patient. I would suggest that we get to the issues.

GEORGE MISCHE
 I am trying to speak
 as a human being to the jury
 who I hope are human beings
 and can understand us
 Will the jury dare to deal
 with the spirit of the law
 and the issues we are talking about
 If not we can expect
 no peace no solutions
 only disorder and riots
 in our country and in the world

     ‘ ‘ ‘ ‘ ‘ ‘ ‘ ‘

*The streets of our country are in turmoil. The universities
are filled with rebelling, rioting students. Communists are
seeking to destroy our country; Russia is threatening us with
her might.*

 *The Republic is in danger; yes, danger from within and
without.*

 *Without law and order, our nation cannot survive. We
shall restore law and order.*

ADOLF HITLER

     ’ ’ ’ ’ ’ ’ ’ ’ ’

DEFENSE
 Mr. Mische, after you left the Alliance for Progress, what
did you do?
GEORGE MISCHE
 I came back to the United States
 and went around this country
 I talked to university students
 I talked to religious groups

I talked at businessmen's clubs
I spoke to 80 Catholic Bishops
As a Catholic I apologize to you
for their cowardice
I asked them
since they have $80 billions worth of property
and ten times as much in investments
If they were really to live
in the spirit of the stable
in which Christ was born
then why not get rid of the buildings
give them to the poor

PROSECUTION
Your honor, may I object again?

JUDGE
We are not trying the Bishops of the United States.

GEORGE MISCHE
It seemed to me that the war in Vietnam
was illegal   because only Congress
can declare a war
The President cannot legally
take us into a war
We should never have let him
He should be on trial here today
In the peace movement
one of the most powerful things I knew of
was Philip Berrigan's first trial
for the blood pouring
A six-year sentence
for pouring blood on files
Men walk our streets
spilling blood continuously
and they walk free
I also had a feeling   a strong feeling
about what happened in Germany during the last war
my father was from Germany
The United States in 1945
supported the Nuremberg trials

I thought   that was the finest precedent
this country ever set
I said   Good   You are right
All of us Christians
share the responsibility
for having put those Jews
in the ovens

‹ ‹ ‹ ‹ ‹ ‹ ‹ ‹ ‹

ACCUSED #12
    Your Honor
    I would like to explain that
    every third word we heard
    even back in grammar school
    was about
    how they
    were to blame for everything
    and how they
    ought to be weeded out
    It was hammered into us
    that this would only be for the good
    of our people
    In leadership school
    we were taught above all
    to accept everything
    without question
    If anybody did raise a question
    they were told
    What is being done
    is done strictly according to the law
    Your Honor
    we weren't supposed to think for ourselves
    There were others around to do our thinking for us

WEISS: THE INVESTIGATION

If this was true
then it is also true
that this is expected of me now
as a Christian
Because the Vietnamese people are crying out
Stop the bombing   Stop the napalming
Stop the death   day in and day out
But now
we want to forget the precedent
we set in 1945
There is a tendency to say
That was another country   another time
It is said
in times of crisis
We cannot make black and white decisions
Everything is gray
That is the problem
It is easy for us on Monday morning
to tell how we should have played
Sunday's game
We say that it is too complicated
It is too obscure
So nothing happens
The violence continues
I felt that the crisis
this country is in
needed something drastic
something people could see
But the act had to be nonviolent
We were not out to destroy life
There is a higher law we are commanded to obey
It takes precedence over human laws
My intent was to follow the higher law
My intent was to save lives   Vietnamese lives
North and South American lives
To stop the madness
That was the intent

PROSECUTION
>   Is it your position that those who take a view contrary
>   to yours are insane?

GEORGE MISCHE
>   No sir   you did not hear
>   I was trying to say
>   that the style of one's action
>   must coincide with the style of his life
>   And that is all

JOHN HOGAN
I have something of a comparison
an analogy
If there were   a group of children
walking along the street
returning home from school
and a car
came down the street
out of control   even though
there was a driver in that car
If I could divert the car
from crashing into those children
I would feel an obligation
to turn the car from its path
Of course the car is property
and would be damaged
It is even possible
something would happen
to the individual in the car
But no matter   I would be thinking
ten times more of those children
than of the driver of that car
And I know too
if I were driving that car
and it were out of control
I would hope
and pray to God
that somebody would smash the car
so that I might not destroy those children

DEFENSE
> If there were, Mr. Hogan, one phrase in which you could
> sum up your intent in going to Catonsville, how would
> you express it?

JOHN HOGAN
> I just want
> to let people live
> That is all

JUDGE
> I did not hear it.

JOHN HOGAN
> I said
> I want to let people live
> That is all

DEFENSE

What was the impact of the act of your brother Philip
Berrigan when he poured blood on draft files in Baltimore?

DANIEL BERRIGAN

I began to understand
one could not indefinitely obey the law
while social conditions deteriorated
structures of compassion breaking down
neighborhoods slowly rotting
the poor despairing   unrest
forever present in the land   especially among
the young people
who are our only hope   our only resource
My brother's action helped me realize
from the beginning   of our republic
good men and women had said no
acted outside the law
when conditions so demanded
And if they so acted
time might vindicate them   show their acts to be lawful
a gift to society
a gift to history
and to the community
A few

must have a long view
must leave history to itself
to interpret their lives   their repute

Someday
these defendants may be summoned
to the Rose Garden and decorated
but not today

DEFENSE

Could you state to the court what your intent was in
burning the draft files?

DANIEL BERRIGAN

I did not want the children
or the grandchildren of the jury
or of the judge
to be burned with napalm

JUDGE

You say your intention was to save these children, of the
jury, of myself, when you burned the records? That is
what I heard you say. I ask if you meant that.

DANIEL BERRIGAN

I meant that
of course I mean that
or I would not say it
The great sinfulness
of modern war is
that it renders concrete things abstract
I do not want to talk
about Americans in general

JUDGE

You cannot think up arguments now that you would
like to have had in your mind then.

DANIEL BERRIGAN

My intention on that day
was
to save the innocent
from death by fire
I was trying to save the poor
who are mainly charged with
dying in this war
I poured napalm
on behalf of the prosecutor's

and the jury's children
It seems to me quite logical
If my way of putting the facts
is inadmissible
then so be it
But I was trying to be concrete
about death   because death
is a concrete fact
as I have throughout my life
tried to be concrete
about the existence of God
Who is not an abstraction
but is someone before me
for Whom I am responsible

DEFENSE

Was your action at Catonsville a way of carrying out
your religious beliefs?

DANIEL BERRIGAN

Of course it was
May I say
if my religious belief is not accepted
as a substantial part of my action
then the action is eviscerated
of all meaning   and I should be
committed for insanity

DEFENSE

How did your views on the Vietnam war take shape?

DANIEL BERRIGAN

My views on war and peace
arose in me slowly
as life itself
pushed hard and fast
I should like to speak of
5 or 6 stages   in my development
I was invited to South Africa
around Easter of 1964
There I had about two weeks
of intense exposure

to a segregationist police state
At one meeting in Durbin
I remember   the question being raised
What happens to our children
if things go so badly
that we have to go to jail?
I remember saying
I could not answer that question
not being a citizen of that country
but I could perhaps help
by reversing the question
What happens to us and our children
if we do *not* go to jail?
2   I visited eastern Europe twice
in 1964
meeting with Christians in Czechoslovakia   Hungary
                                                Russia
This had bearing
on my development   I was coming to realize
what it might cost to be a Christian
what it might cost
even at home
if things were to change
in the direction I felt events were taking
even then
In the summer of 1965   I went to Prague
to attend the Christian Peace Conference
This was a kind of breakthrough
For the first time   a Catholic priest
sat in that vast assembly of Christians
from all over the world   from Marxist countries
from India   from Africa   from the east and west
talking about things
that diplomacy and power and the military
were not talking about
That is to say
How can we survive as human beings
in a world

more and more officially given over
to violence and death
I think the imperceptible movement
of my conscience
was pushed forward by that experience
3   I returned in the summer of 1964
and was assigned as editor and writer
at a magazine in New York
named *Jesuit Missions*
I was quite convinced
that the war in Vietnam
would inevitably worsen
I felt that a cloud
no larger than a man's hand
would shortly cover the sky
In the autumn of 1964
I began to say no to the war
knowing
if I delayed too long
I would never find the courage to say no
In that year
I underwent a rebirth
becoming a peacemaker
in a time of great turmoil
New York was not an auspicious place
to be a peaceable Catholic priest
Cardinal Spellman was living
He had always supported American wars
He believed   I think this states his thought
that the highest expression   of Christian faith
was to bless our military
By his Christmas visits
to our foreign legions
he placed official approval
on our military adventuring
I had to say no to that too
I had to say no to the church

‹ ‹ ‹ ‹ ‹ ‹ ‹ ‹

Gentlemen:
Since we are among those pagans who take declarations
seriously, we must ask you as declared Christians, certain
questions. . . .
Should you not stand up and denounce with all the right-
eousness and pity and anger and charity and love and humil-
ity which your faith may place at your command, the polit-
ical and militarist assumptions now followed by the leaders
of the nations of Christendom?
Pagans are waiting for your answer. You claim to be
Christians. What does that mean as a public fact?

C. WRIGHT MILLS: A PAGAN SERMON

› › › › › › › › ›

4   Finally
in the autumn of 1965
I was exiled from the United States
to Latin America
JUDGE
What do you mean, "exiled"?
DANIEL BERRIGAN
I was sent out   your honor
with no return ticket
As one of my friends expressed it
sending me to Latin America was a little like
tossing Br'er Rabbit into the briar patch
I visited ten countries in four and a half months
from Mexico to Southern Chile and then
up the western coasts
I discussed American involvement
in the political and social scene of those countries
I spent time with the students   the slum dwellers
with whatever government officials would talk
as well as with church leaders
In Mexico   a student said to me

We hate you North Americans   with all our hearts
but we know   that if you do not make it
we all come down   we are all doomed
I arrived in Rio in January of 1966
in the midst of devastating floods
In the space of a single night
the rains came down with torrential force
whole towns collapsed
people and shacks fell into a stew of death
I remember the next morning
slogging through the mud
in the company of a slumdweller
who was also a community organizer
He looked at me and said
My friend   millions for war in Vietnam
and this for us

JUDGE

What? Are you saying that the United States government caused the flood?

DANIEL BERRIGAN

I think   the fact
was a bit more subtle than that
I think he was saying
the resources of America
which belong in justice
to the poor of the world
are squandered in war   and war preparation

DEFENSE

Now may I ask about your writings and publications?

PROSECUTION

What difference does it make how many books he has
written?

DEFENSE

I show you the book *Night Flight to Hanoi.* Will you
outline the circumstances out of which this book was
written?

DANIEL BERRIGAN

5   The book marks

the next stage   of my development
In January of 1968   an invitation came
from the government of North Vietnam
Professor Howard Zinn and myself
were invited to Hanoi
to bring home   3 captive American airmen
For me to go to Hanoi
was a very serious decision
I believe   I have always believed
that the peace movement must not merely say no
to the war
It must also say
yes to life   yes to the possibility of a human future
We must go beyond frontiers
frontiers declared by our country or by the enemy
So I thought it would be important
to show Americans
that we were ready to risk our lives
to bring back American prisoners
because we did not believe
that in wartime
anyone should be in prison
or should suffer separation
from families
simply   we did not believe in war
And so we went

‘ ‘ ‘ ‘ ‘ ‘ ‘ ‘ ‘

What crime have I committed, I keep on asking?
The crime of being devoted to my people.

HO CHI MINH: PRISON DIARY

In Hanoi I think we were the first Americans
to undergo
an American bombing attack
When the burned draft files
were brought into court yesterday
as evidence
I could not but recall
that I had seen in Hanoi
evidence of a very different nature
I saw   not boxes of burned papers
I saw parts of human bodies   preserved in alcohol
the bodies of children   the hearts and organs and limbs
of women

‹ ‹ ‹ ‹ ‹ ‹ ‹ ‹

EVIDENCE FOR THE PROSECUTION

The boxes of paper ash
The size of infant caskets
Were rolled in on a dolly,
Heaped there like cord wood
Or children after a usual
Air strike on Hanoi.
I heard between heartbeats
Of Jesus and his hangman
The children's mouths mewing
For the breasts of murdered women
The blackened hands beating
The box of death for breath.

DANIEL BERRIGAN

, , , , , , , , ,

teachers   workers   peasants   bombed
in fields and churches and schools and hospitals
I examined our "improved weaponry"
It was quite clear to me
during three years of air war

America had been experimenting
upon the bodies of the innocent
We had improved our weapons
on their flesh

JUDGE

He did not see this first hand. He is telling of things he
was told in Hanoi, about some things that were preserved
in alcohol.

DANIEL BERRIGAN

French   English   Swedish experts   doctors
testified
these were actually the bodies
whose pictures
accompanied the exhibits
The evidence was unassailable
The bombings
were a massive crime against man
The meaning of the air war in the North
was the deliberate systematic destruction
of a poor and developing people

JUDGE

We are not trying the air war in North Vietnam.

DANIEL BERRIGAN

I must protest the effort
to discredit me on the stand
I am speaking of what I saw
There is a consistent effort
to say that I did not see it

JUDGE

The best evidence of what some "crime commission"
found is not a summary that you give.

DANIEL BERRIGAN

So be it
In any case we brought the flyers home
I think as a result of the trip to Hanoi
I understood the limits
of what I had done before
and the next step that must come

' ' ' ' ' ' ' ' '

Calamity has tempered and hardened me and turned my
mind to steel.

HO CHI MINH: PRISON DIARY

' ' ' ' ' ' ' ' '

On my return to America
another event
helped me understand
the way I must go
It was the self-immolation
of a high school student
in Syracuse New York
in the spring of 1968
This boy had come to a point of despair
about the war   He had gone
into the Catholic cathedral
drenched himself with kerosene
and immolated himself in the street
He was still living a month later
I was able to gain access to him
I smelled the odor
of burning flesh
And I understood anew
what I had seen in North Vietnam
The boy was dying in torment
his body like a piece of meat
cast upon a grille
He died shortly thereafter

I felt that my senses
had been invaded in a new way
I had understood
the power of death in the modern world
I knew I must speak and act
against death
because this boy's death
was being multiplied
a thousandfold
in the Land of Burning Children
So I went to Catonsville
and burned some papers   because
the burning of children
is inhuman and unbearable
I went to Catonsville
because I had gone to Hanoi
because my brother was a man
and I must be a man
and because
I knew at length
I could not announce the gospel
from a pedestal
I must act as a Christian
sharing the risks and burdens and anguish
of those whose lives were placed
in the breach by us
I saw suddenly   and it struck with the force of light-
ning
that my position was false
I was threatened with verbalizing
my moral substance out of existence
I was placing upon young shoulders
a filthy burden   the original sin of war
I was asking them to enter a ceremony of death
Although I was too old
to carry a draft card   there were other ways
of getting in trouble with a state
that seemed determined upon multiplying the dead

totally intent upon a war
the meaning of which   no sane person could tell
So I went to Hanoi
and then to Catonsville
and that is why I am here
DEFENSE
Did you not write a meditation to accompany the state-
ment issued by the nine defendants at Catonsville?
DANIEL BERRIGAN
Yes sir
DEFENSE
Would you read the meditation?
DANIEL BERRIGAN
Certainly
"Some ten or twelve of us (the number is still uncertain)
will if all goes well (ill?) take our religious bodies
during this week
to a draft center in or near Baltimore
There we shall   of purpose and forethought
remove the 1–A files   sprinkle them in the public street
with home-made napalm   and set them afire
For which act we shall beyond doubt
be placed behind bars for some portion of our natural
                                                                    lives
in consequence of our inability
to live and die content in the plagued city
to say 'peace peace' when there is no peace
to keep the poor poor
the thirsty and hungry thirsty and hungry
Our apologies   good friends
for the fracture of good order   the burning of paper
instead of children   the angering of the orderlies
in the front parlor of the charnel house
We could not   so help us God   do otherwise
For we are sick at heart   our hearts
give us no rest for thinking of the Land of Burning
                                                                    Children
and for thinking of that other Child of whom

the poet Luke speaks   The infant was taken up
in the arms of an old man whose tongue
grew resonant and vatic at the touch of that beauty
And the old man spoke: this child is set
for the fall and rise of many in Israel
a sign that is spoken against
Small consolation   a child born to make trouble
and to die for it   the First Jew (not the last)
to be subject of a 'definitive solution'
And so we stretch out our hands
to our brothers and sisters throughout the world
We who are priests to our fellow priests
All of us who act against the law
turn to the poor of the world   to the Vietnamese
to the victims   to the soldiers who kill and die
for the wrong reasons for no reason at all
because they were so ordered by the authorities
of that public order which is in effect
a massive institutionalized disorder
We say: killing is disorder
life and gentleness and community and unselfishness
is the only order we recognize
For the sake of that order
we risk our liberty   our good name
The time is past when we may be silent
when obedience
can segregate us from public risk
when the poor can die without defense
How many indeed must die
before our voices are heard
how many must be tortured dislocated
starved maddened?
How long must the world's resources
be raped in the service of legalized murder?
When at what point will you say no to this war?
We have chosen to say
with the gift of our liberty
if necessary our lives:

the violence stops here
the death stops here
the suppression of the truth stops here
this war stops here
Redeem the times!
The times are inexpressibly evil
Christians pay conscious   indeed religious tribute
to Caesar and Mars
by the approval of overkill tactics   by brinkmanship
by nuclear liturgies   by racism   by support of gen-
                                                            ocide
They embrace their society with all their heart
and abandon the cross
They pay lip service to Christ
and military service to the powers of death
And yet   and yet   the times are inexhaustibly good
solaced by the courage and hope of many
The truth rules   Christ is not forsaken
In a time of death some
the resisters   those who work hardily for social change
those who preach and embrace the truth
such overcome death
their lives are bathed in the light of the resurrection
the truth has set them free
In the jaws of death
they proclaim their love of brothers and sisters
We think of such men and women

in the world   in our nation   in the churches
and the stone in our breast is dissolved
we take heart once more"
DEFENSE
    Nothing further.

4

The Day of Summation

DEFENSE

Your honor, the government's concession this morning, with reference to the reasonableness of the views held by these defendants, has, in the opinion of the defense, made it unnecessary to call expert witnesses.

Since the government concedes that reasonable men can hold that the war is illegal, unconstitutional, and immoral, the proffered witnesses no longer have any relevance to this case.

PROSECUTION

Your honor, I want it understood for the record that I don't accept his use of the word "concession." If we accept the version of the defense, they would have it believed that the government feels that any person who thinks the war in Vietnam is illegal would be insane. We never took this position, so there is no concession to make.

DEFENSE

Your honor, I might indicate that the government has never before publicly made the statement that was made in this court today. There is a great difference between saying that "a man is insane to hold these views," and saying, "a reasonable man can hold these views."

JUDGE

The government certainly is not conceding that those views are correct, and the court will have to rule on those as a matter of law. And that is the test case that you want.

DEFENSE

I am making the record clear. The argument now is not the correctness of the views, but whether a reasonable man could hold them. . . .

JUDGE

At any rate, the defense has its test case. Now I ask: Is the government ready to begin the final argument?

PROSECUTION

The government is ready, your honor.

May it please the court and members of the jury. It is now my responsibility to attempt, in summary fashion, to review with you the evidence that has been produced in this courtroom.

First of all, I want it clearly understood that the government is not about to put itself in the position—has not heretofore and is not now—of conducting its policies at the end of a string tied to the consciences of these nine defendants. This trial does not include the issues of the Vietnam conflict. It does not include the issue of whether the United States ought to be in the conflict or out of it.

The government quite candidly admits that the position these defendants took is reasonable—as to the fact that the war is illegal, that it is immoral, that it is against religious principles, that any reasonable man could take that view. We do not even say that a person has to be insane to have the views that they have. No, we don't say that.

But this prosecution is the government's response, the law's response, the people's response, to what the defendants did. And what they did was to take government property and throw flammable material upon it and burn it beyond recognition. And that is what this case is about.

There are people, it hardly need be pointed out, who rely upon the files in Local Board No. 33 in Catonsville.

Suppose you were to acquit these people on the only basis possible, in view of everything they have conceded? Acquit them, that is, although they did those acts with the intention of hindering the Selective Service System and of burning the files and records. Suppose that because of their sincerity, their conscience, their religious convictions, they were entitled to be acquitted in this courtroom?

If these people were entitled to be acquitted by virtue of their sincerity and religion and conviction, then according to the same logic, should not the man who commits any other crime be also entitled to acquittal?

We also heard about unpleasant things happening, or about to happen, in other areas of the world. Among these nine defendants, there are four or five justifications floating around. One defendant is upset about one ill in the world, and that justifies his going to Catonsville. Another is upset about another ill in the world, and that justifies his going to Catonsville. And so on. The possibilities are infinite. There could in fact be fifty defendants, each upset about fifty different supposed ills in the world. And each one of them could say: This is why I violated the law.

Ladies and gentlemen of the jury, the government has never contended that this country is perfect, that it is without flaw, without ills and problems and failings. To assert that would be absurd.

But I would suggest to you that, to the extent that this country has problems, those problems will be solved. We will progress. We will get better. The country will get better.

But our problems are not going to be solved by people who deliberately violate our laws, the foundation and support for an ordered and just and civilized society.

It is your sworn duty to assert, by finding the defendants guilty, that our problems will not be solved, but will be increased beyond imagining, by people who deliberately violate the law under which we all live.

ʿ ʿ ʿ ʿ ʿ ʿ ʿ ʿ ʿ

Whatever commandment the prisoner has disobeyed is writ-
ten upon his body by the Harrow. This prisoner for instance
(the officer indicated the man) will have written on his
body: HONOR THY SUPERIORS.

KAFKA: THE PENAL COLONY

, , , , , , , , ,

DEFENSE

Ladies and gentlemen of the jury, this is an historic moment for all of us—for the judge, the jury, the counsel,
the defendants. Undoubtedly, a great measure of personal
reflection is required, even to begin to appreciate the
meaning of this trial for us who participated in it.

As for those who did not, only the passage of time
can tell whether the events of this courtroom will strike
responsive chords both in our country and around the
world.

I must beg your leave to inject a personal note. In law
school, I was repeatedly warned never to identify too
closely with prospective clients. Perhaps under other circumstances, this might be considered sound advice. But
as your honor acknowledged during the trial, these are
not ordinary clients; and this is hardly a run-of-the-mill
prosecution.

For myself, I must confess with more heartfelt pride
than I could adequately describe, that in the course of
this litigation, I have come to love and respect the men
and women who stand before this court. Like them, I
make no plea for mercy. I dare not tarnish the transcend-
ent witness they have given, in an attempt to persuade
this court to bend in their direction.

Still, there are some things I must say if I am to remain faithful to my obligations as a lawyer, as an American, and as a human being.

The court has agreed that this is a unique case. It shares the historic meaning of other great contests of law. The trial of Socrates was not merely a question of a man sowing confusion and distrust among the youth of Athens; the trial of Jesus could not be reduced to one of conspiracy against the Empire.

In a parallel way, there are overriding issues at stake in this case; I hope to bring them to your attention, within the limits the defense is allowed to touch on.

In the first place, we agree with the prosecutor as to the essential facts of the case. The defendants did participate in the burning of records.

You must have understood, because it was pointed out here, that the Selective Service System is an arm of the Federal government, for the procurement of young men for military service, as decided by the authorities of the United States.

In other words, such young men are to be used, as one defendant said, for cannon fodder, if the government so dictates.

It is not a question of records which are independent of life. We are not talking about driving licenses or licenses to operate a brewery. We are speaking of one kind of records. No others so directly affect life and death on a mass scale, as do these. They affect every mother's son who is registered with any Board. These records stand quite literally for life and death to young men.

The defendants did not go to Catonsville to act as criminals, to frighten Mrs. Murphy, or to annoy or hinder her. They were there to complete a symbolic act (first of all) which we claim is a free speech act. And secondly, they were there to impede and interfere with the operation of a system which they have concluded (and it is not an unreasonable belief, as the government has told you) is immoral, illegal, and is destroying innocent people around the world.

The defendants weren't burning files for the sake of burning files. If they were, I would not stand in this

court to defend them. They burned the files at Catonsville for two reasons, both of which they admitted:

They wanted, in some small way, to throw a road-
block into a system which they considered murderous,
which was grinding young men, many thousands of them,
to death in Vietnam.

Also, they wanted, as they said, to reach the American public, to reach you. They were trying to make an
outcry, an anguished outcry, to reach the American community before it was too late. It was a cry that could
conceivably have been made in Germany in 1931 and
1932, if there were someone to listen and act on it. It
was a cry of despair and anguish and hope, all at the
same time. And to make this outcry, they were willing
to risk years of their lives.

The government has conceded that the defendants
were sincere, it has conceded their truthfulness. The
government has also conceded that it is reasonable to
hold the views held by the defendants as to the illegality
of this war.

So we come to the only issue left for you to decide:
whether, in your opinion, they are guilty or innocent of
crime.

I want to point out to you, in some detail, a case
which offers parallels to this one, a case which affected
the character of American history, some two hundred
years ago. The defendant was a printer, Peter Zenger by
name; he was accused of seditious libel. Andrew Hamilton, the defending lawyer, spoke the following words in
the course of the trial (it seems to me that they are of
point here).

"Jurors are to see with their own eyes, to hear with
their own ears, and to make use of their conscience and
understanding in judging of the lives, liberties, and es-
tates of their fellow subjects."

Ladies and gentlemen of the jury, that is what we are
asking you to do.

JUDGE

You are urging the jury to make their decision on the basis of conscience. This morning, I said to you that if you attempt to argue that the jury has the power to decide this case on the basis of conscience, the court will interrupt to tell the jury their duty. The jury may not decide this case on the basis of the conscience of the defendants. They are to decide this case only on the basis of the facts presented by both sides.

‹ ‹ ‹ ‹ ‹ ‹ ‹ ‹

Put simply, the court said, the right to be tried by a jury of one's peers . . . would be meaningless, if the judge could call the turn. . . . In the exercise of its function, not only must the jury be free from direct control of its verdict, it must be free from judicial pressure, both contemporaneous and subsequent.

U.S. COURT OF APPEALS, REVERSING
THE CONVICTION OF DR. SPOCK

› › › › › › › › ›

DEFENSE

I would like to say to the jury: I am appealing to you, as Andrew Hamilton appealed to a jury, to consider all the facts of the case before you.

All the words, writing, marching, fasting, demonstrating—all the peaceable acts of the defendants, over a period of some years—had failed to change a single American decision in Vietnam. All their protests had failed to prevent a single innocent death, failed to end the anguish of napalm on human flesh, failed even momentarily to slow the unnatural, senseless destruction of men, women, and children, including the destruction of our own sons—a destruction wrought in the name of a policy that passes all human understanding.

Perhaps in the last analysis, this cataclysm of our times can be understood only in the lives of a few men who, for one moment, stand naked before the horrified gaze of their fellow men.

Anne Frank did this for six million Jews. And it may be that the thousands of American and Vietnamese ghosts created by this war can best be spoken for by three small children who crouched in a Hanoi air raid shelter, before the compassionate eyes of an American priest.

He saw in these children, as many of us saw in Anne Frank, the waifs spawned by an incomprehensible and savage war; a war that envelops and affects each of us, and makes us partners in the common tragedy which brings me before you.

Perhaps in this poem by Daniel Berrigan, who stands in judgment before you, some understanding of the truth of things can come through.

"Imagine; three of them.

As though survival
were a rat's word
and a rat's end
waited there at the end

and I must have
in the century's boneyard
heft of flesh and bone in my arms

I picked up the littlest
a boy, his face
breaded with rice (his sister calmly feeding him
as we climbed down)

In my arms fathered

in a moment's grace, the messiah
of all my tears. I bore, reborn

a Hiroshima child from hell."

JUDGE
The jury may now begin their deliberations.

(*The jury files out.*)

Now then, let the defendants or their counsel be
heard from. Have I said something I should not have
said, or left unsaid something I should have said?
DEFENSE
Your honor, the defendants have requested to be per-
mitted to say something to the court.

(*Whereupon, at this point, the following proceedings were
had.*)

5

The Day of the Verdict

JUDGE

I want to hear the defendants. I do not want to cut them off from anything they may want to say. Mr. Melville, will you begin?

THOMAS MELVILLE

Your honor, we feel that the overriding issue in the case has been obscured by the treatment given us. If our intention was to destroy government records, we could very easily have gone in at nighttime and taken the files out and burned them.

As it was, we went in the middle of the day, and, after burning the files, waited for fifteen minutes until the police came, to give public witness to what we did.

Our intention was to speak to our country, to the conscience of our people.

Now, during these few days we have been in this court in an attempt to speak to the conscience of the American people. We feel that the twelve jurors have heard all kinds of legal arguments, which I suppose they must hear. But we feel that the overriding issue has been obscured. You have sent the jury out—to judge whether we committed the acts which we admitted from the beginning that we had committed.

JUDGE

The jury are not the representatives of the American people. Also, nobody has cut you down on the evidence you wanted to present. You have made your case in public.

It is quite true that I have not submitted to the jury the question you would like to have submitted, in a way you would like. I have told the jury if they find that you intended to burn the records and hinder the draft board, then it was immaterial that you had other good purposes. And it was immaterial how sincere you were and how right you may ultimately be judged by history.

I am not questioning the morality of what you did.

I disagree with the theory of law which you are presenting and which was argued very eloquently by your counsel, as far as I would permit him to do it. I cannot allow somebody to argue something which is entirely contrary to the law. That would be to ask the jury to disregard their oath. I cannot allow that.

If you had gone to Catonsville and taken one file under some token arrangement, you might have had something to argue. But you went out and burned 378 files, according to your own admission. And every one of you, I think, said that you did it in order to hinder the operation of the draft.

I am not questioning the highness of your motive. I think that one must admire a person who is willing to suffer for his beliefs. But people who are going to violate the law in order to make a point must expect to be convicted.

THOMAS MELVILLE

Your honor, we are not arguing from a purely legal standpoint. We are arguing to you as an American, with your obligations to society, to those jurors as Americans and in their obligations to our society.

If it is only a question of whether we committed this act or not, we feel it would be better if the jury is dismissed. We can save ourselves a lot of time and money by receiving an immediate sentence from you.

JUDGE

Mr. Mische next.

GEORGE MISCHE

My question, your honor, concerns conscience. Did you tell the jury they could not act according to their conscience?

JUDGE

I did not mention conscience.

‘ ‘ ‘ ‘ ‘ ‘ ‘ ‘

JUDGE

I said this to the defense: If you attempt to argue that the jury has the power to decide this case on the basis of conscience, the court will interrupt and tell the jury of their duty.

COURT RECORD

, , , , , , , , ,

I did not talk about conscience. I do not mind saying that this is the first time the question of conscience has been raised in this court.

GEORGE MISCHE

But was the jury told they could not use their conscience in determining—

JUDGE

I certainly did not tell them they could disregard their oath and let you off on sympathy, or because they thought you were sincere people.

DANIEL BERRIGAN

Your honor, we are having great difficulty in trying to adjust to the atmosphere of a court from which the world is excluded, and the events that brought us here are excluded deliberately, by the charge to the jury.

JUDGE

They were not excluded. The question—

DANIEL BERRIGAN

May I continue? Our moral passion was excluded. It is as though we were subjects of an autopsy, were being dismembered by people who wondered whether or not we had a soul. We are sure that we have a soul. It is our soul that brought us here. It is our soul that got us in trouble. It is our conception of man.

But our moral passion is banished from this court. It is as though the legal process were an autopsy.

JUDGE

Well, I cannot match your poetic language.

(*Applause from the audience.*)

Any further demonstration and the court will be cleared. And I mean that, the whole crowd.

Father Berrigan, you made your points on the stand, very persuasively. I admire you as a poet. But I think you simply do not understand the function of a court.

DANIEL BERRIGAN

I am sure that is true.

JUDGE

You admitted that you went to Catonsville with a purpose which requires your conviction. You wrote your purpose down in advance. Your counsel stood and boasted of it. Now I happen to have a job in which I am bound by an oath of office.

If you had done this thing in many countries of the world, you would not be standing here. You would have been in your coffins long ago. Now, nobody is going to draw and quarter you. You may be convicted by the jury; and if you are, I certainly propose to give you every opportunity to say what you want.

DANIEL BERRIGAN

Your honor, you spoke very movingly of your understanding of what it is to be a judge. I wish to ask whether or not reverence for the law does not also require a judge to interpret and adjust the law to the needs of people here and now. I believe that no tradition can remain a mere dead inheritance. It is a living inheritance which we must continue to offer to the living.

So it may be possible, even though the law excludes certain important questions of conscience, to include them none the less; and thereby, to bring the tradition to life again for the sake of the people.

JUDGE

Well, I think there are two answers to that. You speak to me as a man and as a judge. As a man, I would be a very funny sort if I were not moved by your sincerity on the stand, and by your views. I agree with you completely, as a person. We can never accomplish what we would like to accomplish, or give a better life to people, if we are going to keep on spending so much money for war. But a variety of circumstances makes it most difficult to have your point of view presented. It is very unfortunate, but the issue of the war cannot be presented as sharply as you would like. The basic principle of our law is that we do things in an orderly fashion. People cannot take the law into their own hands.

DANIEL BERRIGAN

You are including our President in that assertion.

JUDGE

Of course, the President must obey the law.

THOMAS LEWIS

He hasn't though.

JUDGE

If the President has not obeyed the law, there is very little that can be done.

GEORGE MISCHE

And that is what this trial is all about. . . .

DANIEL BERRIGAN

Your honor, you have referred to the war question as one which may be either political or legal. Suppose it were considered as a question of life and death. Could that be appropriately raised here?

JUDGE

Well, again, that is poetic speech. I am not sure what the legal proposition is. I understand why it seems a matter of life and death to you. Of course, the war is a matter of life and death to all boys who are in it. It is a matter of life and death to people in Vietnam.

MARY MOYLAN

Your honor, I think you said previously that you had a great deal of respect for the law and the Constitution of the United States.

I would like to call this respect into question, if you are unwilling to do anything about a war which is in violation of our legal tradition and the United States Constitution.

JUDGE

Well, I understand your point. But I cannot appoint you either my legal or spiritual adviser.

GEORGE MISCHE

We have people from the peace movement here. Will you, then, allow them to file in your court, calling into question the entire Vietnam war; and will you be willing to review the charge in its entirety? Whatever decision you make then can be submitted to the Supreme Court.

JUDGE

But you have to have a case—

GEORGE MISCHE

You have to break a law first.

JUDGE

—that can be brought in court.

GEORGE MISCHE

You have to break a law. It seems that, before we can get a judge to face the situation, you have to break a law, as Dr. King found.

JUDGE

If you had gotten legal advice, I am sure you would have been advised that there are better ways to raise this question than the way you raised it at Catonsville.

THOMAS LEWIS
Your honor, one question:
I have been called an honest and just man in this
courtroom. I appreciate that. But the reality is that I
leave this room in chains. I am taken back to prison.
How do you explain this?

JUDGE
Good character is not a defense for breaking the law.
That is the only way I can explain it.

DAVID DARST
Your honor, the instructions you gave to the jury bound
them to the narrow letter of the law. And a verdict according to the spirit of the law was strictly prohibited.
It is my feeling that the spirit of the law is important,
particularly in American legal tradition and in American
life. It is the spirit which counts.

JUDGE
I am not God almighty. I did what the law required me
to do. All we can do is our best. . . .

PHILIP BERRIGAN
Your honor, I think that we would be less than honest
with you if we did not state our attitude. Simply, we have
lost confidence in the institutions of this country, including our own churches.
I think this has been a rational process on our part.
We have come to our conclusion slowly and painfully.
We have lost confidence, because we do not believe any
longer that these institutions are reformable.

JUDGE
Well, if you are saying that you are advocating revolution—

＊ ＊ ＊ ＊ ＊ ＊ ＊ ＊

*Whenever the ends of government are perverted and public
liberty manifestly endangered and all other means of redress
are ineffectual, the people may, and of right ought to, reform*

the old or establish a new government. The doctrine of non-resistance against arbitrary power and oppression is absurd, slavish, and destructive of the good and happiness of mankind.

CONSTITUTION OF THE STATE OF NEW HAMPSHIRE,
ARTICLE 10

, , , , , , , , ,

PHILIP BERRIGAN

I am saying merely this:

We see no evidence that the institutions of this country, including our own churches, are able to provide the type of change that justice calls for, not only in this country, but around the world.

We believe that this has occurred because law is no longer serving the needs of the people; which is a pretty good definition of morality.

JUDGE

I can understand how you feel. I think the only difference between us is that I believe the institutions can do what you believe they cannot do.

PHILIP BERRIGAN

Our question remains: How much time is left this country, as our casualties inch upward, as Vietnamese casualties mount every day? And nuclear war is staring us in the face. That is the question we are concerned about: man's survival.

JUDGE

I assure you I am concerned about your question, for my grandchildren, as well as for everybody else. It is a serious thing.

GEORGE MISCHE

Change could come if one judge would rule on the war. If one judge would act, the war could not continue as it does.

JUDGE

I think you misunderstand the organization of the United States. One judge ruling on it would not end the war. Each judge must do his best with what comes before him. . . .

DANIEL BERRIGAN

We want to thank you, your honor; I speak for the others. But we do not want the edge taken off what we have tried to say, by any implication that we are seeking mercy in this Court. We welcome the rigors of the Court.

Our intention in appearing here after Catonsville was to be useful to the poor of the world, to the Black people of the world and of our country, and to those in our prisons who have no voice.

We do not wish that primary blade of intention to be honed down to no edge at all by a gentleman's agreement, whereby you agree with us and we with you. We do not agree with you, and we thank you.

JUDGE

All right.

DANIEL BERRIGAN

Could we finish with a prayer? Would that be against your wishes? We would like to recite the "Our Father" with our friends.

JUDGE

The Court has no objection whatsoever, and rather welcomes the idea.

(*Whereupon, at this point in the proceedings, those who wished to do so stood and joined in prayer.*)

JUDGE

(After 1½ hours) I have just received a note from the foreman. The jury has concluded its deliberations and is ready to report its findings. The jury will come in now, and the clerk will take the verdict.

There must be no demonstrations from the audience. If there are, I may clear the room, or I may instruct the marshal to take appropriate action with respect to any recalcitrants.

(Whereupon at this point the jury was brought into the courtroom, and the following proceedings were had.)

THE CLERK

The taking of the verdict in Criminal Action No. 28111, the United States of America against Philip Berrigan, Daniel Berrigan, Thomas Lewis, James Darst, John Hogan, Marjorie Melville, Thomas Melville, George Mische, and Mary Moylan.

Members of the jury, what say you: Is the defendant John Hogan guilty of the matters whereof he stands indicted?

THE FOREMAN

We find John Hogan guilty.

THE CLERK

Members of the jury, what say you: Is the defendant Marjorie Melville guilty of the matters whereof she stands indicted, or not guilty?

THE FOREMAN

We find Marjorie Melville guilty.

THE CLERK

Members of the jury, what say you: Is the defendant Thomas Melville guilty of the matters whereof he stands indicted, or not guilty?

THE FOREMAN

We find Thomas Melville guilty.

THE CLERK

Members of the jury, what say you: Is the defendant George Mische guilty or not guilty of the matters whereof he stands indicted?

THE FOREMAN

We find George Mische guilty.

THE CLERK

Members of the jury, what say you: Is the defendant

Mary Moylan guilty of the matters whereof she stands
indicted, or not guilty?

THE FOREMAN

We find Mary Moylan guilty.

THE CLERK

Members of the jury, what say you: Is the defendant
Philip Berrigan guilty of the matters whereof he stands
indicted, or not guilty?

THE FOREMAN

We find Philip Berrigan guilty.

THE CLERK

Members of the jury, what say you: Is the defendant
Daniel Berrigan guilty of the matters whereof he stands
indicted, or not guilty?

THE FOREMAN

We find Daniel Berrigan guilty.

THE CLERK

Members of the jury, what say you: Is the defendant
Thomas Lewis guilty of the matters whereof he stands
indicted, or not guilty?

THE FOREMAN

We find Thomas Lewis guilty.

THE CLERK

Members of the jury, what say you: Is the defendant
James Darst guilty of the matters whereof he stands indicted, or not guilty?

THE FOREMAN

We find James Darst guilty.

A MEMBER OF THE AUDIENCE

Members of the jury, you have just found Jesus Christ
guilty.

(*Commotion in court. Similar outbursts from other members of the audience.*)

JUDGE

Marshals, clear the coutroom.

(*Whereupon, at this point the courtroom was slowly cleared.*)

JUDGE

Now, is there anything further that the government or the defendants wish brought to the attention of the court?

DANIEL BERRIGAN

We would simply like to thank the Court and the prosecution. We agree that this is the greatest day of our lives.

THE VERDICT

Everything before was a great lie.
Illusion, distemper, the judge's eye
Negro and Jew for rigorists.
The children die
Singing in the furnace. In Hell they say
Heaven is a great lie.
Years, years ago
My mother moves in youth. In her
I move, too, to birth, to youth, to this.
The judge's tic-toc is time's steel hand
Summoning
Come priest to the temple. Everything else
Is a great lie. Four walls, home, youth
Truth untried, all all is a great lie.
The truth
The judge shuts in his two eyes
Come Jesuit, the university cannot
No nor the universe, nor murdered Jesus
Imagine. Imagine! Everything before
Was a great lie.
Philip; your freedom, stature
Simplicity, the ghetto where the children
Malinger, die.
Judge Thomsen, strike with a hot hammer
The hour, the truth. The truth has birth
All former truth must die. Everything
Before—faith, hope, love itself
Was a great lie.

DANIEL BERRIGAN

FIRST AFTERWORD
MORE TIMELY THAN EVER: GIVING VOICE TO A
JESUIT EDUCATION FOR PEACE AND JUSTICE

For several reasons, I am delighted that Fordham University Press is publishing a new edition of Daniel Berrigan's *The Trial of the Catonsville Nine*. I consider Berrigan to be one of the few outstanding human beings of the twentieth century and one of the great Jesuits of the last four hundred years. One of my several reasons for making this claim is that his literary, moral, political, and religious witness for justice against injustice is reminiscent of Søren Kierkegaard's critique of Danish Christendom in the nineteenth century. Kierkegaard protested the over-identification of Christianity with the Danish state and economy and claimed that he wished to remind Christians of the difficulty of being Christian.

In a similar way, Berrigan in *The Trial of the Catonsville Nine* and other works warns Catholics and the broader Christian and religious community of the dangers of an over-identification of Christian conscience with the American war-making, money-making state and economy. This reminder came as the Catholic Church in the 1960s was moving away from being a ghetto church and moving towards a cozy relationship with mainstream America and the secular city. John Kennedy's presidency instantiates and symbolizes such a tendency, but Berrigan cautions and warns us about it. What if the United States government and economy is engaging in unjust, imperial domination and exploitation all over the world, and what if the war in Vietnam is an instance of such involvement? Should that be celebrated and praised, or mourned and resisted? And if we opt for the latter, as Berrigan's play suggests that we should, then our lives as human beings and Christians are going to be more difficult, not easier. Following Christ means following Him in a discipleship committed to justice, solidarity with the poor and oppressed, and prophetic resistance and critique, not a comfortable life of upward mobility, consumerism, and social conformity, baptized Catholic and confirmed American.

I am also pleased about the new edition of the play because I have used it regularly in a course about peace and justice the last several years, and I now will have more convenient and easy access to the book. After an inquiry into the national and international aspects of the U.S. state, economy, and culture, in which I use several other texts, the students read out loud in class *The Trial of the Catonsville Nine* as a final text, and we have a discussion the last day of class. What kind of lifestyle, policy, and action does the text suggest that we should follow, after a semester of theoretical reflection on issues of peace and justice?

What emerges from the text and our discussion of it is this kind of question, related to and flowing from the dilemma of the 1960s noted above. "How does one live as a human being, citizen, professional, and Christian of conscience in the midst of the most virulent empire in the history of the world?" The U.S.–led empire, it could be argued, is virtually worldwide and is unparalleled in its destructiveness to the environment, injustice towards peoples, support of terrorist third-world regimes, and direct or indirect structural engendering of massive poverty, unemployment, hunger, and disease. For example, over 20 million people die per year from hunger in domains under our direct or indirect control, and over 10 million people a year die from diseases that could be easily treated with a fraction of the wealth that U.S. banks and corporations take out of these countries every year. In its destructiveness, extent, and devastation inflicted on people and nature, the U.S.–led empire, it could be argued, makes ancient empires like Persia or Rome or even early twentieth-century empires like those of Great Britain or Germany seem relatively benign by comparison.

The students in the class are encouraged to respond, question, agree, or disagree with the play, each from the perspective of her own conservative, liberal, or radical conscience. Not everyone ends up agreeing with the conclusion of the play, but some do, and many others find their values, lives, and conduct changing as they reflect upon the import of the play. The play functions as a Socratic challenge in the best sense. Perhaps, I suggest, even if one is not called to a civil disobedience similar to that undertaken by the nine people in the play, we need to ask what it means to translate the spirit and values of the play into one's life as a human being and Christian. What are the implications for the choice of a mate, of a profession, the way one lives out and practices that profession, and the way one lives out her life as a citizen and Christian?

The play has much contemporary pertinence and resonance—more, I would argue, than when it was written. In making this point, I wish to turn to some of the words of Daniel Berrigan in his *The Trial of the Catonsville Nine*. In dialogue attributed to himself, he says:

> Our apologies   good friends
> for the fracture of good order   the burning of paper
> instead of children   the angering of the orderlies
> in the front parlor of the charnel house
> We could not   so help us God   do otherwise
> For we are sick at heart   our hearts
> give us no rest for thinking of the Land of Burning Children
> and for thinking of that other Child of whom
> the poet Luke speaks. (93–94)

These words of Berrigan are doubly prophetic: first, about the injustice of the Vietnam War, and, second, about the kind of nation the U.S. was more and more turning into—more militaristic, consumeristic, exploitative, and imperialistic. And who can deny that, forty or so years later, we have become, or are several further steps along the way to becoming, precisely the kind of nation he is warning us against. Two wars in the Gulf, the self-contradictory terrorist war against terrorism in Afghanistan, and the intervention in Kosovo are indications of this point. The U.S. and the U.S.–led empire have within their grasp worldwide domination, hegemony, exploitation.

Berrigan's play points to the warning not heeded, a road not taken, a choice not made. And yet all is not lost. Although

> The times are inexpressibly evil
> Christians pay conscious   indeed religious tribute
> to Caesar and Mars
> by the approval of overkill tactics   by brinkmanship
> by nuclear liturgies   by racism   by support of gen-
> ocide
> They embrace their society with all their heart
> and abandon the cross
> They pay lip service to Christ
> and military service to the powers of death
> And yet   and yet   the times are inexhaustibly good
> solaced by the courage and hope of many
> The truth rules   Christ is not forsaken
> In a time of death some
> the resistors   those who work hardily for social change
> those who preach and embrace the truth
> such overcome death
> their lives are bathed in the light of resurrection
> the truth has set them free (95)

Past, present and future readers of this book can be or become such men and women. Prior to and during the war in Iraq, thousands of protests involving millions of people occurred all over the world in what may have been the most impressive expression of moral conscience in human history. And such protest has not ceased but is ongoing. It is to the emergence of a fully human world pointed to by those protests, the road thus far not taken, that the play contributes.

—James L. Marsh

Works Cited

Albert, Michael. *Stop the Killing Train.* Boston: South End Press, 1994: 76.

Nelson-Pallmeyer, Jack. *Brave New World Order.* Maryknoll, NY: Orbis Books, 1992: 4–5.

SECOND AFTERWORD
THEN AND NOW: NOTES ON THE HISTORICAL
SIGNIFICANCE OF THE TRIAL OF THE
CATONSVILLE NINE

On May 17, 1968, when the Catonsville Nine burned 378 draft files with napalm, the picture of Kim Phuc running from flames had not yet been taken. It would be four long years and many more bombs before the image of the little Vietnamese girl who stripped off her clothes trying to rid herself of napalm jelly would be seen around the world. Phan Thi Kim Phuc was one of millions, but she became the most recognizable face that expressed the horrors of the Vietnam War. Mary Moylan went to Catonsville as a nurse who had worked in Africa, a person dedicated to saving lives. The effects of napalm were real to her long before Kim's picture was published, not a distant, incomprehensible horror. She thought of the children and women "burned alive by a substance which does not roll off. It is a jelly. It adheres. It continues burning." (65)

The Catonsville Nine chose to use a homemade version of napalm for symbolic as well as practical reasons. They didn't create a jelly, rather they left the lethal substance in liquid form, better suited for turning its deadly purpose against itself: burning the papers, files, and records of the faceless management of human destruction. As David Darst testifies in *The Trial of the Catonsville Nine*, "on the records which gave war and violence their cruel legitimacy." (34)

Kim Phuc became the visual icon of the human cost of the Vietnam War, and over the years her image has evoked grief, pain, sorrow, and guilt, but also interpretation and revision. In the years that followed, much has been made of the fact that the incident was an "accident." The plane that bombed Kim and killed her two cousins on June 8, 1972, was flown by a Vietnamese pilot in support of South Vietnamese troops. They were fighting the North Vietnamese Army after it occupied the village of Trang Bang. The pilot bombed the South Vietnamese children in "error." The news media incorrectly reported at the time that an American commander had ordered the air strike, but the United States military maintains that no Americans were involved in the incident.

Debate over the details of the photograph and its taking are motivated by a desire for absolution as much as a need for accuracy. The deliberation also invites a type of intellectual distance from the initial emotional response to the image. If the burning of Kim was "unintentional," carried out in error, then the call to war can somehow gain back some of its "cruel legitimacy." If death is "accidental" it becomes acceptable. In these terms, war can be planned and justified, relied on and perpetuated, as it continues to be.

With the war on Iraq, the media habitually depicted the killing of people as "inadvertent," never a logical consequence of war. As the military planned a violent campaign in the densely populated city of Baghdad, the media helped make those plans acceptable to the public. Consider the language and logic of NBC correspondent Jim Miklaszewski as he reported on February 9, 2003, that the Pentagon was worried about the possible "thousands" of Iraqi civilians that may "be killed entirely by accident in an intensive bombing campaign." When bombs are dropped on a city, the people living there will be killed. How can the result of such planning be "accidental" death?

One way that the myth of death as an unintended consequence of war is perpetuated is through another rhetorical construction of modern warfare—the celebration of high-tech weaponry. Indeed, the state of the art of American weaponry confers, ironically, a moral legitimacy on the battles and bombs that are "smart," "precise," and "deadly accurate," but only to the intended targets. The depictions of war as unintentional, while at the same time precise, stand awkwardly side-by-side in a language that seeks to mitigate the contradiction. On March 21, 2003, one month after explaining that accidents could happen, NBC's Miklaszewski would use the military phrase "surgical strike," saying, "every weapon is precision-guided—deadly accurate, designed to kill only the targets, not innocent civilians." Rachel Coen and Peter Hart, writing in the media criticism journal *EXTRA!* (2003, 17) point out, "The view that all the U.S.'s weapons are 'precise' would seem to be at odds with the notion that all civilian deaths caused by U.S. attacks are 'accidents,' but both claims were equally popular with the U.S. press." The refusal to admit the logical consequences of the weapons of war reveals the social amnesia required for a public to accept state killing in its name.

In January 1968, Daniel Berrigan and Howard Zinn rejected acquiescence to the war and went to Hanoi. There they saw firsthand the effects of American bombs on the people of Vietnam. As Berrigan testifies in *The Trial of the Catonsville Nine* (the actual trial took place in October of 1968), "teachers, workers, peasants—bombed, in fields and churches and schools and hospitals. I examined our 'improved weaponry.' It was quite clear to me during three years of air war America had been experimenting upon the bodies of the innocent. We had improved our weapons on their flesh." (89–90) Demonstrating that diplomacy provided an alternative to violence, Zinn and Berrigan successfully negotiated the release of three American airmen held captive in North Vietnam.

During times of war, the social amnesia required to accept war's killing is referred to as "public resolve," or to use the World War I phrase, "homefront morale." The public's "resolve" to continue a conflict depends on a complicated equation that compares the war's justification to its destructive force. Once the public perceives that the cost in human life is too high a price to pay for the stated goals, opinion turns against further killing.

The courage of the Catonsville Nine and the many others who rejected the war helped bring home the collective realization that thousands of American soldiers had been killed and that Vietnamese deaths would be in the millions. The American military lost the battle over public perception in a stunning defeat. In the minds of the public, the prolonged war that became a "quagmire" could not justify the loss of life. Presidents and generals have since called the rejection of war the "Vietnam syndrome," and as the term implies, it is viewed as a disease, a set of symptoms, a disorder. Those who perpetuate war now understand that images and activism, if allowed to be seen and heard, can stop the violence of war. Vietnam reaffirmed that war in the information age demands a symbolic environment that denies the human costs and assures the public that accepting war is just and morally legitimate. During the war in Iraq, television commentators helped convince audiences that military actions and modern weaponry worked better than diplomacy, that war was the only way. Retired General Barry McCaffrey is only one of many ex-generals now paid as a TV analyst. On MSNBC March 31, 2003, McCaffrey openly idolized the weapons of war: "Thank God for the Abrams tank and the, you know, the Bradley fighting vehicle. The war isn't over until we've got a tank sitting on top of Saddam's bunker." In addition to his fee from NBC, McCaffrey has other financial interests in war. As *The Nation* pointed out in their March 21, 2003, issue, he sits on the board of Integrated Defense Technologies, a company that in March alone "received more that $14 million worth of contracts relating to Abrams and Bradley machinery parts and support hardware." The words of Thomas Lewis in *The Trial of the Catonsville Nine* in Baltimore Federal Court are as true today as they were then; only the weapons systems have changed:

> The Sentinel Missile System
> would not be possible if it were not for this war
> Who are gaining from the war?
> They are an elite minority
> who are very wealthy
> But what is happening to the poor
> in this country?

(47)

In the twenty-first century, America is a brave new world where those who profit from weapons are now also paid to persuade the public of their virtues. And the war economy continues to transfer money from the mouths of babes into the pockets of military contractors.[1]

Thirty-five years after the events depicted in *The Trial of the Catonsville Nine*, one in five children goes to bed hungry in America as Halliburton and the Carlyle Group make millions on the war.

In place of social and economic justice, a virtual culture of thrills and glory regales viewers with an adrenaline rush of dramatic conflict. As U.S. troops pressed into Iraq, the made-for-TV war merged news with cinematic references and reality-show camera angles. Viewers gazed across the sand from inside army vehicles in fantasy ride-alongs with desert warriors as tanks and armored convoys sped "virtually unopposed deep into the Iraqi desert." (CNN, March 21, 2003) Camera and journalistic perspectives merged into a point of view united with the military effort. Empowered by riding shotgun with the soldiers, many journalists barely contained their excitement. They wore goggles and flak jackets and even reported through gas masks as they adopted military jargon: "There are boots on the ground." They interviewed "Top Gun" pilots and crawled along the ground with gunfire in the distance, pressing microphones into soldiers' faces as they pointed their weapons. So surreal was the experience that newscasters felt compelled to tell viewers that the images they were seeing were live, not a movie.

As he helped turn war into entertainment, Tom Brokaw admitted its effects: "Television cannot ever adequately convey the sheer brute force of war, the noise and utter violence." (*New York Times*, March 23, 2003) Certainly not, when violence and brutality are edited out, as excitement and heroics are sensationalized. But Mr. Brokaw passed blame to the medium itself. "It somehow gets filtered through the TV screen, and that's probably just as well,"

In this virtual video culture, no one ever dies on the other

1. For a discussion of the effects of military spending on funding for social programs and entitlements, see Brouwer, 1998. Another graphic display of the distribution of wealth and public moneys can be found in Heintz and Folbre; see chapter 5 for a discussion of military spending.

side of the screen. The high-tech thrills are disassociated from the killing of real people. Creating a new TV genre for war is a process of distancing the public from experiencing emotional empathy or responsibility for war's victims. Though they were in the thousands, Iraqi civilian deaths were all but ignored in the American media, especially on television, a sharp contrast to the international press and Internet Web sites. Equally disturbing, the few reported were contextualized in ways that blocked compassion or accountability. Over sixty people were killed when a missile crashed into a heavily populated open-air market in the Shuala section of Baghdad. The media avoided assigning blame for the deaths. The *New York Times* reporting was typical: "it was impossible to determine the cause." (March 29, 2003) By May 2003, no U.S. news outlets had reported investigations into the bombing, but British war correspondent Robert Fiske found a serial number on a missile fragment at the scene of the explosion. The London newspaper, the *Independent*, traced the number to the Raytheon Corporation. The number corresponded to the HARM anti-radar missile or a Paveway laser-guided bomb—both American weapons used in the bombing. The *Independent* determined that the damage to the market was consistent with a HARM missile, which has a tendency to go off-target.

One U.S. newsmagazine (*Newsweek*, April 7, 2003) asserted that it did not matter who was responsible. "In at least one respect, it doesn't make much difference who bombed the two markets. Either way, Iraqis are blaming the Americans, and Saddam Hussein is reinforcing his position among his people." In this view, people killed by the not-so-smart weapons gain significance only as pawns of abstract strategy; the same article declares, "When it comes to manipulating the minds of his countrymen, Saddam Hussein is a malevolent genius." What are the spiritual consequences visited upon a public encouraged to respond with hatred for "the enemy" instead of sorrow for war's victims? As Dan Berrigan asks in *The Trial of the Catonsville Nine*, "How can we survive as human beings in a world more and more officially given over to violence and death?" (84–85)

Already victimized by the terrorist attacks of September 11,

2001, the American public has been further assailed by fearful government rhetoric and unsubstantiated claims left unchallenged by the U.S. media. Americans are the only ones in the world who believe the now-discredited link between Saddam Hussein and al-Qaeda. In the aftermath of the terrorist attacks, public fear and anger were cynically directed toward retaliation and fantasies of revenge. The enemy was "wanted dead or alive." In a speech on October 7, 2002, George Bush stated, "We've learned that Iraq has trained al-Qaeda members in bomb-making and poisons and deadly gases. . . . Alliance with terrorists could allow the Iraqi regime to attack America without leaving any fingerprints." In fact, no evidence of such a connection has ever been produced. Secretary of State Colin Powell repeated the allegations in a speech to the United Nations, asserting that al-Qaeda training took place in a camp in northern Iraq. "To his great embarrassment, the area he indicated was later revealed to be outside Iraq's control and patrolled by Allied war planes." (Scheer 2003, 2)

Those who remember the Gulf of Tonkin resolution were not so easily fooled by the Bush administration's justifications for the Iraq war. President Lyndon Johnson was given the power to make war in Vietnam after he announced to Congress that American ships on "routine patrol" had been attacked. It is now well documented that every element of that claim was false. For the Catonsville Nine, the killing in Vietnam was never justified. In the words of Daniel Berrigan in the play, "All of us who act against the law turn to the poor of the world—to the Vietnamese—to the victims—to the soldiers who kill and die for the wrong reasons, for no reasons at all, because they were so ordered by the authorities, of that public order which is in effect, a massive institutionalized disorder." (94)

As the media celebrated the victory over Iraq with endless replays of the image of Saddam Hussein's statue pulled to the ground, every one of the stated reasons for the war on Iraq began to unravel. The triumphal celebrations overcame war's truths as victory sought to erase public conscience. "The picture says something about us as Americans," pronounced USA

Today (March 10, 2003), "about our can-do spirit, our belief in lending a hand." The *Washington Post's* Ceci Connelly, interviewed on Fox News (April 9, 2003), was one of many to compare it to the tearing down of the Berlin Wall: "Just sort of that pure emotional expression, not choreographed, not stage-managed, the way so many things these days seem to be. Really breathtaking."

Only a few reporters pointed out the ways in which the event was stage-managed. "Whenever the cameras pulled back, they revealed a relatively small crowd at the statue," the *Boston Globe* noted (April 10, 2003); others were struck by the fortuitous appearance on the scene of a pre–Gulf War Iraqi flag at Firdos Square. Indeed, as the war drags on, American soldiers have become an army of occupation and continue to be at risk, ambushed by Iraqis who clearly did not view the invasion as liberation.

The power of images to mold perceptions created a type of intolerance for the truth characteristic of the poisoned atmosphere of "homefront morale." As Ron Martz, a print journalist for the *Atlanta Journal-Constitution* wrote in *Editor and Publisher*, "When I wrote in one story about 'bloody street fighting in Baghdad,' it appeared the morning TV viewers were seeing jubilant Marines and Iraqi civilians tearing down statues of Saddam Hussein on the eastern side of the Tigris River. Some readers, believing all of Baghdad was like that, were livid. They did not grasp the fact that, on the western side of the river, pitched battles were still taking place. Because they did not see it on TV, it was not happening. And it did not fit their view of the war." By the end of the day, noted *Chicago Tribune* television critic Steve Johnson (April 10, 2003), "the symbol's power had overtaken the hard facts."

Basking in such glories, it seemed irrelevant that no weapons of mass destruction had been found. CIA director George Tenet admitted that the agency should not have allowed the president to claim in his State of the Union Address that Hussein had weapons of mass destruction—the documents had been forged. As Howard Zinn (2003, 2) notes "The so-called 'drones-of-death' turned out to be model airplanes. What Colin Powell called 'decontamination trucks' were found to be fire trucks. What U.S. leaders called 'mobile germ labs' were found by an official British inspection team to be used for inflating artillery balloons." Admitting to a profound "institutionalized disorder," U.S. Deputy Defense Secretary Paul Wolfowitz, one of the main architects of the war, explained why it was necessary to make such claims. He stated in an interview with *Vanity Fair* (May 2003) that "for reasons that have a lot to do with the U.S. government bureaucracy, we settled on the one issue that everyone could agree on: weapons of mass destruction."

Yet even as the war was executed and celebrated, 27 percent of the public remained opposed to it, but those views were silenced. A study of network news done by F.A.I.R. (Rendall and Broughel, 2003) showed that less than 3 percent of U.S. sources on TV expressed views against the war. Real people were about ten times more likely to oppose the war than those seen on television.

What do people of conscience do when their government carries out an unjust war in the name of its citizens, even as it closes down democratic forms of debate and expression? In a democracy, how can killing that is denied and hidden be stopped? Is a just society possible when the fictions of war become more believable than the death left in its wake?

On October 6, 2001, the day before the Bush Administration began bombing Afghanistan, three Dominican sisters entered the inner enclosure of a Minuteman III missile silo in Greeley, Colorado. In a symbolic act of protest, they poured their blood in the shape of crosses on the walls and on the tracks that would be used to guide the huge 110-ton concrete lid open for a launch of the nuclear weapon. One of the nuns, Sister Ardeth Platte, explained, "The Minuteman III is ten times more powerful than the bomb that killed 150,000 people in Hiroshima. President Bush had said repeatedly that he would use nuclear weapons as a first strike." To enter the silo, Sister Ardeth, along with Sisters Jackie Hudson and Carole Gilbert, cut holes in two chain-link fences that surround the missile site designated N8. For this act, property damage was estimated at over $1,000.

As the women in northeastern Colorado beat on the concrete housing of the missile with ball-peen hammers, their action of civil resistance could be traced directly back to Catonsville. The long continuum from the Vietnam War to the new wars of the twenty-first century contains within it the actions of people whose convictions demand resistance to war and its weapons. As Dan Berrigan explains in *The Trial of the Catonsville Nine*, "We could not—so help us God—do otherwise. For we are sick at heart—our hearts give us no rest for thinking of the Land of Burning Children." (93) It was the power of those convictions that pushed Marjorie Melville to Catonsville, even knowing that the cost would be high. "I did not want to bring hurt upon myself, but there comes a moment when you decide that some things should not be. Then you have to act to try to stop those things." (58) Just as Sister Carol, explaining why she chose to protest her government's radical new foreign policy of "preemptive strikes," felt compelled to enter the missile silo and draw attention to the inconceivable power of a "bomb that will destroy every living thing in a fifty-mile radius, it doesn't distinguish between children, women, or men."

After Catonsville, Philip Berrigan continued to resist the Vietnam War, and with his wife Elizabeth McAlister founded the "resistance community" Jonah House, in 1973. Inspired by Isaiah 2:4 "to beat swords into plowshares," the Plowshares Movement was begun in 1980.[2] Shortly before his death on December 6, 2002, Phil Berrigan linked the Catonsville action to his continued protest against the inhumanity of weapons of mass destruction: "I die with the conviction, held since 1968 and Catonsville, that nuclear weapons are the scourge of the earth; to mine for them, manufacture them, deploy them, use them, is a curse against God, the human family, and the earth itself." (O'Neill 2002, 13) Though members of the Jonah House community, Sisters Carol and Ardeth were in jail when Philip Berrigan died.

After the Catonsville trial, as Daniel prepared to give up

2. For complete documentation of the Plowshares Movement, see www.plowsharesactions.org.

his freedom, Howard Zinn wrote, "Dan Berrigan is facing prison because he (and his brother Phil, and others) decided to protest the mass murder of the Vietnam War by destroying draft card files in Baltimore. Of course he violated the law. But he was right. And it is the mark of enlightened citizens in a democracy that they know the difference between law and justice, between what is legal and what is right." (Zinn 1996, 66) Those who listen to the higher call of which Zinn speaks often pay dearly in a social order determined to solve its problems through the weapons of war. As Dan Berrigan remembered the life of his brother, he acknowledged the high cost of frequent incarcerations. Philip, he said, "learned patience through bolts and bars, through stopped clocks and time served, at the icy hands of judges and guards and wardens. He learned it through the war-making state and the complicit church, through long sacrifice and small return, through 35 years of American war and scarcely a week of genuine peace. . . . Patience was like an iron yoke placed on his shoulder." (O'Neill 2002, 13)

In the late 1960s, many Catholics lived with the contradictions of a church leadership too timid to oppose a brutal war. Only later would Daniel Berrigan's own religious order, the Jesuits, recognize the importance of his long commitment to peace. In 1996, in a tribute to Father Berrigan on his 75th birthday, Peter-Hans Kolvenbach, S.J., the superior general of the Society of Jesus, wrote, "Our world continues to be ravaged by war, starvation, poverty, and oppression. The international sale of weapons promotes the death of millions. The ongoing maintenance of nuclear weapons in the face of massive poverty and hunger remains a crime against God and humanity." (Kolvenbach 1996, 163) He went on to assert that "Christian conviction demands that we be people of peace, people who insist that a world without war is possible. And so, it is right that we celebrate Father Daniel Berrigan, because peace took root in his heart. . . ." (Kolvenbach 1996, 164)

For those who fight for peace in America, our country imposes ever-harsher penalties. For the symbolic act against the Minuteman III, the three nuns were convicted of sabotage, even though two Air Force colonels, both prosecution witnesses, testified that the "women had never interfered with or obstructed national defense." (Nieves 2003, A1) The nun's lawyers told the *Washington Post* that sentencing guidelines of five to ten years would constitute "one of the harshest punishments ever handed down for what amounts to a trespassing case in which the gravest damage was to a piece of chain-link fence." (Nieves 2003, A1)

A columnist for the *Denver Post* recognized the absurdity of such a sentence: "If this constitutes homeland security in post–September 11th America, the watchdog needs dentures. When they're not protesting for peace, the nuns teach in poor neighborhoods, helping the least of us. Locking them up is like locking up Mother Teresa. It's just wrong." (Spencer 2003) When thousands of letters were sent to the court demanding leniency, the churchwomen were sentenced to two-and-a-half to three-and-a-half years—still considered by many to be an extremely harsh sentence for a symbolic act of peace.

How long will we as a country allow the most courageous among us to suffer such retaliation at the hands of the state? How can we consider ourselves a civilized and enlightened people in face of the actions against those who bring acts of injustice and brutality to our attention? How can democracy survive if we acquiesce to the persecution of voices critical of our government's actions and policies?

A group of students, the Fordham Experimental Theater, performed *The Trial of the Catonsville Nine* on the Bronx campus of Fordham University in the spring of 2003. Their production included a set decorated with the words from the play. The only poem adorning the theater's walls not included in the Catonsville text was this one:

> Let America be the dream the dreamers dreamed—
> Let it be the great strong land of love
> Where never kings connive nor tyrant scheme
> That any man be crushed by one above.
> (It never was America to me.)[3]

These sentiments surround those social critics and visionaries, the Hughes and Berrigans in our midst, those brave

---

3. "Let America Be America Again" by Langston Hughes.

enough to inspire us and challenge America to be another
America, the one that many dream is possible.

> We have chosen to say
> With the gift of our liberty
> If necessary our lives:
> The violence stops here
> The death stops here
> The suppression of truth stops here
> This war stops here
> Redeem the Times!

(94–95)

This remains the message and the challenge of *The Trial
of The Catonsville Nine.*

—Robin Andersen
September 2003

WORKS CITED

Brouwer, Steve. *Sharing the Pie: A Citizen's Guide to Wealth
and Power in America.* New York: Henry Holt and Company, 1998.

Coen, Rachel and Peter Hart. "Brushing Aside the Pentagon's
'Accidents': U.S. Media minimized, sanitized Iraq War's
civilian toll." *EXTRA!* (May/June 2003): 17–18.

Heintz, James and Nancy Folbre. *The Ultimate Field Guide to
the US Economy.* New York: The New Press, 2000.

Kolvenbach, S. J., Peter-Hans. "Servant of Christ's Mission in
a World of War." *Apostle of Peace: Essays in honor of Daniel Berrigan,* John Dear, ed. New York: Orbis Books, 1996.

Martz, Ron. "Embed Catches Heat: TV Sanitized the Iraq
Conflict, But a Paper Gets the Hate Mail." *Editor and Pub-
lisher.com* (May 15, 2003).

Nieves, Evelyn. "For Three Nuns, A Prairie Protest And a Price
to Pay: Sisters Reconciled to Prison For Action at Missile
Site." *Washington Post* (May 21, 2003): A-1.

O'Neill, Patrick. "A Tribute to Philip Berrigan 1923–2002. *The*

Sign of Peace: The Journal of the Catholic Peace Fellowship (Vol. 2, 1, 2002): 13.

Rendall, Steve and Tara Broughel. "Amplifying Officials, Squelching Dissent: FAIR Study Finds Democracy Poorly Served by War Coverage." *EXTRA!* (May/June):12–14.

Scheer, Christopher. "Ten Appalling Lies We Were Told About Iraq." AlterNet.org (June 27).

Spencer, Jim. "Locking up nuns makes sense to none." *The Denver Post* (July 17, 2003).

Zinn, Howard. "The Specter of Vietnam." TomPaine.com (June 26, 2003).

——— "Peace Pilgrim to Vietnam," *Apostle of Peace: Essays in honor of Daniel Berrigan.* John Dear, ed. New York: Orbis Books, 1996.